CHRISTIAN ETHICS AND THE DILEMMAS OF FOREIGN POLICY

CHRISTIAN ETHICS AND THE
DILEMMAS OF FOREIGN POLICY

Kenneth W. Thompson

PUBLISHED FOR THE LILLY ENDOWMENT RESEARCH
PROGRAM IN CHRISTIANITY AND POLITICS BY THE
DUKE UNIVERSITY PRESS, DURHAM, N. C.   1959

Printed in the United States of America

Dedicated
to
My Mother
A Teacher of Christian Ethics
by
Example

Foreword

The formulation of foreign policy and the conduct of foreign relations are probably the most crucial areas of political decision and activity in the contemporary world. We have heard a great deal about the importance of bringing our moral commitments to bear upon these areas of political activity but something more than moral exhortation is required if our moral commitments are to be meaningfully related to the problems now confronting our statesmen. Dr. Thompson concentrates his attention in this book upon three such problems: armaments, colonialism, and diplomacy. In analyzing the difficulties encountered in relating moral principles, and especially Christian moral principles, to problems of this kind Dr. Thompson draws upon the experience of statesmen like Churchill and Bismarck, of diplomatists like George F. Kennan and Dean Acheson, and historians like Herbert Butterfield and Geoffrey Barraclough. He is not content, however, simply to analyze what others have done and said but endeavors to elucidate and defend a critical view of his own.

Kenneth W. Thompson is well-qualified to undertake this task. He was trained as a political scientist and taught in that field at the University of Chicago and at Northwestern University. He is currently serving as Associate Director for Social Sciences at the Rockefeller Foundation in New York City. He has been a frequent contributor to the professional journals and is the co-author of *Principles and Problems of International Politics* (1952); *Man and Modern Society* (1954); *Isolation and Security* (1957) and *Foreign Policy in World Politics* (1958). He is a member of the Editorial Board of *International Organization* and of *Christianity and Crisis*.

The present volume is based upon a series of three lectures which Dr. Thompson delivered at Duke University in March, 1959 under the auspices of the Lilly Endowment Research Program in Christianity and Politics.

It should be understood, of course, that although the publication of this book was made possible by funds provided by Lilly Endowment, Inc., the Endowment is not the author or publisher and is not to be understood as approving, by virtue of its grant, any of the statements or views expressed in the pages that follow.

John H. Hallowell, *Director*

Lilly Endowment Research Program in Christianity and Politics

Preface

This little volume reflects a long-term interest in the inter-relationships of Christian ethics and foreign policy. It represents a furrow I hope to plow more deeply in years to come. I have endeavored to approach my subject in the spirit of free inquiry and independent thought—long a hallmark of the western tradition. The Lilly Endowment Program at Duke University, and particularly Professor John Hallowell, prompted and encouraged the lectures on which the book is based. I am grateful, as a part-time scholar, to Professor Hallowell for providing the necessary incentive for sustained intellectual endeavor. It goes without saying that he and his colleagues are in no sense responsible for the defects of thought or presentation in the book—failings for which I alone must be held accountable.

I am especially grateful to the Rockefeller Foundation and its President, Dean Rusk, for allowing me to prepare and deliver the lectures, to my wife and children for their patient and forgiving spirit when research and writing invaded family days, and to my parents who early gave me the moral guidance and intellectual stimulation that led in the direction of these problems. The completion of the manuscript would not have been possible without the extraordinary skill and devotion of Mrs. Elena Amirian and Mrs. Ethel Williams.

Kenneth W. Thompson

Table of Contents

CHRISTIAN ETHICS AND THE DILEMMAS OF FOREIGN POLICY

Chapter One

MORAL IMPERATIVES AND THE AMBIGUITIES OF INTERNATIONAL LIFE

> "If the democratic nations fail, their failure must be partly attributed to the faulty strategy of idealists who have too many illusions when they face realists who have too little conscience."—REINHOLD NIEBUHR

May I begin with a word about the purpose of this little volume. The first choice that anyone pretentious enough to discuss the relationship of Judaeo-Christian precepts and foreign policy must make is the spirit or attitude in which he shall approach his subject. When he turns for advice or counsel to others, their guidance is often opposing and mutually contradictory. One school maintains that the student of such a question should divest himself of any trace of commitment or personal belief. The best of modern social science, we are told, is value-free. It is science because it is bereft of misleading prejudice or preconception that would lead to a predetermined end. The observer worth his salt in science must start with a *tabula rasa* on which events and phenomena are free to write their own story. The opposite school of thought, however, enjoins the scholar to keep his aim and purpose ever before him and before those who hear or read his words. If it is the ideal of the United Nations he seeks to implant, he must allow neither facts nor the ordering of events ultimately to deter him from his goal. If democracy, religious faith, or law and justice be his purpose, his task once again is to arrange what he says primarily to instil convictions and values conducive to these aims.

The present discourse will be directed to a target somewhere between the two extremes. On one hand, I believe that value-free social science, except for the most restricted, narrow, and frequently insignificant subjects, tends to be an absurdity and an illusion. It may be useful in testing limited areas of consumer behavior, political attitudes, or population trends. However, the great and timeless literature on man's social behavior is permeated by goals and purpose. *On Liberty,* the *Federalist Papers,* and *A History of the English-Speaking People,* to select at random three great writings from the classical and present-day world, share the intent of both informing and inspiring the reader. One need not aspire to join the select company of John Stuart Mill, James Madison, Alexander Hamilton, and Winston S. Churchill to affirm that belief in a burning human goal or a clear social purpose is, for any social inquiry, a legitimate point of departure. It so happens that I begin with the proposition that one of our supreme tasks in foreign policy is to bring moral purpose and political realities into line and to understand their relationship more deeply and in terms that carry meaning for men in other lands. However, I believe that this overarching goal can be subjected to intellectual discipline, can be safeguarded at once from cynical nihilism or hypocritical moralism, and can be measured or played against the living standards of international political behavior. I believe that morality as distinct from moralism can be discovered and analyzed in international affairs as in other social realms.

I am emboldened to make this claim partly because of the image of social science I find most convincing. Social science as I see it is no aimless venture but at taproot a purposeful undertaking. Even in rigorous science, a felt need or social purpose is oftentimes the first step in the direction of progress. In the physical sciences, we are told that the demands for better health led to the creation of medical science just as the need for roads and bridges laid the groundwork for engineering. The weight of evidence in the history of science suggests that a social or technical need may be a greater spur than many universities. Research for the sake of amassing data or thinking for thinking's sake is as often barren as not. By contrast, the sensitive observer confronted by a basic problem is challenged to order his questions and direct his answers to some crucial point. According to the German philosopher Kant, reason approaches nature "not in the character of a pupil, who listens to all that his master chooses to tell him, but in that of a judge, who compels the witness to reply to those questions which he himself thinks fit to propose." International relations in this sense is no exception, for it has passed through successive stages in which scholars of note chose to emphasize the questions that reality imposed upon them. New realities in the present day call for new insights as well.

Having pointed up the unity of all science and its source in controlling questions, propositions, and ideas, I must also call attention to an important distinction and offer a warning. The laboratory scientist may possess the same emotions toward the eradication of cancer as the political scientist does toward the elimination of war. But for the laboratory scientist the emotions are strictly irrelevant to and separable from the investigation, since in the physical world the facts exist independently of what anyone may think of them. However, for the social investigator the facts may be changed by the desire that they be changed, for their existence is never wholly independent of his attitude or of the attitudes of those he seeks to influence. The purpose of the social observer is itself one of the facts as such inasmuch as every political or social judgment tends to modify or rearrange the facts on which that judgment is based. For example, the aim of present-day observers of capitalism—including many socialists—is the preservation and defense of capitalism. While Marx maintained he was the founder of a new science and Marxism owes to its scientific pretensions much of its driving power, his approach to the analysis of capitalism was inseparably linked to his goal of destroying capitalism. The same was true of Professor Kinsey, who brought to his research the all-consuming purpose of changing legislation on sex behavior. Those who point to a vital social need or the necessity of solving a problem unquestionably perform a valuable function. They run the risk, however, like the Utopian socialists whom Engels criticized for believing that "socialism is the expression of absolute truth, reason and justice, and needs only to be discovered in order to conquer all the world," of resting content with answers that are partly the fruits of the questions they have asked.

The laboratory scientist may dedicate himself to eliminating cancer, but his dedication does not alter the facts of his experiment. In quite another fashion, the purpose and position of the social observer intimately shape and affect his research. The observer of capitalism, for example, must have some kind of moral and intellectual position concerning his subject, and it is this position which intermingles with his analysis and indeed gives it meaning and purpose.

The risk is of course undeniable that social scientists may feel compelled to hurry the results of their inquiries into forms most immediately applicable to practice. My colleague, Dr. Robert S. Morison, Director of the Medical and Natural Sciences Program of The Rockefeller Foundation, in a paper, "Support of Basic Research From Private Philanthropy," presented on May 15, 1959, to the Symposium on Basic Research at The Rockefeller Institute, has warned that practical motivation has its pitfalls. This brilliant and versatile scientist writes: "It seems particularly difficult for man to study his own behavior without succumbing to the . . . temptation to put his partial knowledge to immediate practical use." He points to Machiavelli, whose findings took the form of handbooks for princes rather than "objective scientific reports"; Ricardo, whose papers on inflation and the Corn Laws led to parliamentary discussion and action; and Jevons, who was not only an outstanding nineteenth-century theoretician, but who contributed "practical papers on the price of gold and the coal question." Dr. Morison concludes by asking whether modest progress in social sciences compared with the phenomenal advances of natural science "is in part due to their own error of emphasizing applied at the expense of basic research."

There are two comments the social scientist can make to this. First, is it in fact true that social science has been so backward in its findings and discoveries? What about social inventions such as the written constitution, the contract in law, the advances of the democratic state, the secret ballot, the welfare state, or the Supreme Court? Are these inventions to be considered inferior to all physical advances? Second, what are we to think of the theoretical significance of a De Tocqueville, a Plato or an Aristotle, or Chief Justice John Marshall, compared with the work of the various institutes of behavioral science? Is there an equal risk of equating basic research with a fairly limited and not yet overwhelmingly superior type of social investigation? I believe there is. Nevertheless, anyone who turns to analyze the moral aspects of international politics must be steady and clear that he is forever surrounded by the manifold dimensions of this problem. He looks at the moral question inevitably from the ground on which he stands. Political theories in effect are advice on how to act. They are always within a system and are arranged around the facts of the situation. If an American were a Guatemalan, he would possibly construct another theory. Or historically as an American or a European, he might in some other period of Western history have put other values higher in his hierarchy of ends. This has been an inescapable reality for almost every historical era.

1. *A Brief Historical Note on the Problem*

Let me illustrate the point by a brief historical survey. Until recent times the bulk of the writing on international morality fell to the international lawyers. While political theory goes back to the speculations of Plato, philosophies of interstate relations are largely embedded in international law. De Tocqueville struck this note in his presidential address to the Academie des Sciences et Politiques when he found for the international realm the sole equivalent to the writings of Plato, Aristotle, Montesquieu, and Rousseau on the rights of society and the individual in those who "undertake the same task with regard to the society of nations in which each people is a citizen—a society always rather barbarous, even in the most civilized periods—and whatever is done to appease and regulate the relations of those who compose it." The prototypes of this latter approach were the classical lawyers like Grotius, Vattel, and Pufendorf. Not the state, as with Plato, but relations among states in the half-organized, half-chaotic interstate realm, was their subject.

The development of the science of international law was concomitant with the breakup of Western Christendom. The task then of publicists and writers was either to salvage from the old or to put something in its place. The publicists of the late Middle Ages chose to demonstrate that legal and moral bonds drawing together all peoples of Western Christendom still existed. There were remnants of a once dominant medieval unity in the institutions of a single ecclesiastical organization. The Papacy with varying effectiveness asserted its authority primarily with respect to things spiritual but, particularly in the late Middle Ages from the latter part of the eleventh to the early fourteenth centuries, with an impact on things temporal as well. The Church, not the Empire, comprehended the moral universe. Moreover, upon the moral foundations of Western Christendom, what in effect constituted an international state sprang up. One publicist noted: "By the time of Innocent III the Church had everything a state had—and more." He could point to canon laws applied by ecclesiastical courts, influence on constitutional questions like succession of states and rulers, responsibility for education and charity, a centralized organization that confirmed "international" agreements, powers of sanction and enforcement like excommunication and the interdict, and the right to protect subjects against unjust treatment by secular rulers. The Church through its *plenitudo potestatis* intervened intermittently to shape and mold events in the temporal realm. Since there was no widely effective political unity, the *Respublica Christianum* possessed both moral and political oneness almost entirely alien to the present fragmented modern state system.

The moral problem lay not in searching out accepted higher standards that transcended partial or parochial loyalties. In this respect the moral dilemma of the day differed from our own. Today political, moral, and religious writers seek some form of higher order, whether in ecumenical movements, the building of common functional interests, or the UN system. Then, however, a higher realm of natural law was already in being. Hence the moral dilemma of the late Middle Ages took root not in the absence of moral unity but in the clash of two contradictory principles. On one hand, the legitimacy or authority of the spiritual order, or "state," was rooted in its expression of Christian love and impartial justice. Its fulfilment was linked with an avoidance of power struggles in the temporal realm where rulers had to compromise with justice. On the other hand, if the Christian society were to have any practical relevance for peace and

order, it had no choice but to intervene. The notion of a
ratio divina clashed head on with the necessity of speaking
and acting in the realm of politics and positive law. As soon
as the line separating the spiritual from the temporal was
breached, all the perennial problems of morality in practical
politics came to the surface. Popes as statesmen might be
children of light but they were acting in the shadowy and
ambiguous realm inhabited by the children of darkness. At
this point the moral dilemma emerged, harassing and pla-
guing saints no less than sinners, and absolute justice became
the victim of ambition, pride, and the force of individual
and collective self-interest. The locus and nature of the problem was to change in succeeding centuries, but the sources
and roots of the dilemma were much the same.

By the seventeenth century, Grotius, as the "Father of the
Science of International Law," was required to substitute
universal natural law for the one ecclesiastical order. For
Grotius, justice was writ large in the universe, no less within
man himself than in society. The one true Church no longer
had a claim to direct influence in world affairs; not common
religious principles but the law of nature bound men ir-
respective of national allegiances to one another. In Grotius'
terms, "The law of nature is a dictate of right reason, which
points out that an act, according as it is or is not in conform-
ity with rational nature, has in it a quality of moral baseness
or moral necessity; and that, in consequence, such an act is
either forbidden or enjoined by the author of nature, God."
Man is driven to achieve not exclusively his own advantage
but the maintenance of the social order. Up to a point at
least, even states in their conduct are not immune to certain
immutable laws. They have the obligation to come to the
aid of another if its cause is just; and, contrariwise, even a
firm alliance cannot require them to help if an ally's actions
are unjust. Moreover, subjects of another state may be defended against an unjust ruler. States can intervene to remedy

a wrong for which no redress is possible for the citizens of another state.

The natural law order, however, is never fully realized or realizable in positive municipal or international law. In effect, positive law is the compromise natural law makes with reality. The actual or historical behavior of states requires adjustment and adaptation of the "self-evident" principles of right reason. In state relations, Grotius was quick to see that "certainty is not to be found in moral questions in the same degree as mathematical science." The *jus gentium* among states introduces the element of consent and custom through which laws lose their quality of fixed realities but become better adapted to existing circumstances and the demands of time and place. States in practice are not expected to join in a "just war" for others if it is prejudicial to their own interests. Moreover, legal consequences may flow even from unjust actions. Thus peace treaties may be valid even though one of the parties is compelled or coerced into giving its consent. To undo legal and political conditions brought about in the course of an unjust conflict would create evils greater than the recognition of changes that come about through fear and force. Grotius believed that pure natural law would always be just beyond reach, and law by consent would endure as long as there were sovereign states. Nonetheless, consent itself derives its validity, as does positive international law, from underlying natural law. While natural law would never be a workable scheme for the international order as it existed, it undergirds volitional law and provides an ultimate point of reference. It remains the great-grandmother of municipal law even though, for the latter, expediency plays a more substantial role.

From Grotius to the present, the stress in a fundamental way has been on positive law. With the notable exception of the somewhat hesitant and uncertain invoking of concepts such as "principles of law generally recognized by civilized nations," as in the Nuremburg trials, faith in an identifiable higher natural law has tended to disappear. Punitive wars in the cause of justice, at least until fairly recent times, have fallen more and more into disfavor. The signs of the transition are present in a writer like Pufendorf, who argued, "For a person to thrust himself forward as a kind of arbitrator of human affairs, is opposed . . . to the equality granted by nature, not to mention the fact that such a thing could easily lead to great abuse, since there is scarcely a man living against whom this could not serve as an excuse for war." Political tests of action, such as the balance of power, come to supplant more absolute guides, such as aid to the oppressed. If states are to act against an unjust aggressor, those with most immediate security interests must be expected to shoulder the major responsibility and burden. Thus politics and interest become the essential guides to state action and a "necessary law of nations" replaces the law of nature. Even the necessary principles of law that to a degree are traceable to residual standards of universal justice are solely the law of the older Christian states of Europe. With other "less civilized states," publicists accept the predominance of "politics over morality." This state of affairs is one with which present-day writers must grapple. The devolution of higher legal and moral principles would seem to be a central fact of the times. Because reasonable and just behavior has not prevailed, power and political considerations have become ever more prominent.

2. Some Contemporary Light on the Problem

The setting in which we face the problems of international life today bears little resemblance to the late medieval or early modern period. Religiously, we enjoy not the benefits of ecclesiastical union but the fruits of separatism and diversity. Legally, the sufficiency of contemporary international law is questioned even by its ardent protagonists. The context in which relations between ethics and international politics work themselves out is best illustrated by the philosophies of three prominent Western leaders. One is an international jurist, perhaps the wisest of our day. Another has been called America's foremost Protestant theologian. The third must be counted among the West's most important statesmen of any age or people. I suggest we examine the thought of these three extraordinary contemporary minds.

Judge Charles de Visscher of Belgium, Catholic philosopher and former member of the International Court of Justice, is more widely known in Europe than on the American continent. An English translation of his classic work, *Theory and Reality in Public International Law,* brought him closer to American writers; recently, the American Society of International Law singled out this treatise as the most important publication of the year. Some go so far as to compare its importance to the writings of Grotius and Vattel. If students of international law and morality were to distil from De Visscher the essence of his philosophy, they would probably include the following elements:

First, the world hopes for but does not possess genuine world community. Despite modern communications and the unifying compulsion of Western technology, there are pitifully few basic solidarities in the present international order. Ironically, the mass media have the effect of making national communities more autonomous, homogeneous, and exclusive than at any time in history. The collective societies around the globe that feed on the products of a nation-wide press, radio, and television network run the inevitable risk of thinking the same thoughts, despising the same enemies, and falling victim to the same unifying slogans. In spite of greater literacy or travel, they do not necessarily become more tolerant, understanding, or compassionate toward foreign peoples, although for parts of the population, a deeper sympathy and understanding is palpably realizable. The modern nation-state in contact with the harsh realities of the external world tends to become more cohesive, more conscious of itself and its problems, and more resistant to unifying forces outside its boundaries. The imperatives of national survival demand greater unity for a single people huddling together within national boundaries that protect it against extinction. Even the Soviet threat, for example, is a spur to better American science, education, and production, not a stimulus to greater world-wide achievements in these fields. International society, lacking in dominant incentives to greater solidarity, substitutes for them a call for sacrifice and the appeal to a common supranational good, but this attainment does not seem open to the great majority of mankind. For most of the newer nations, the margin of their resources, even broadly conceived, is barely sufficient for national survival. The pursuit of a common good is a luxury in which they cannot indulge themselves. To mention three examples, the struggling North African states in the Maghreb (Tunisia, Morocco, and eventually Algeria) dream of not one but three national universities. In all of Latin America no first-class training center for diplomats or central bankers can be found, perhaps because nearly every "republic" aspires to have one of its own. And in the supposedly more developed states, the "fourth country" drive for thermonuclear weapons has already become a burning issue, as in France, Switzerland, and Sweden. In the nation-state, it is the most highly political experiences and the claims of vital interest that evoke supreme solidarities. In the international realm, the opposite is true, for here one finds minor solidarities of an economic or technical order. The nearer the approach to vital questions like the preservation of peace and the prevention of war, the less influence the nascent world community has on its members. "If the international community, or more accurately the sense of such a community, finds so little echo in individual consciences, this is less because power obstructs it than because the immense majority of men are still infinitely less accessible to the doubtless real but certainly remote solidarities that it evokes than to the immediate and tangible solidarities that impose themselves upon them in the framework of national life." [1]

Secondly, Judge de Visscher firmly believes that "neither politics nor law will ensure equilibrium and peace in the world without the 'moral infrastructure.'" Neither positive law walled off from its philosophical or moral roots nor a highly abstract natural law which in any case the contemporary Western World has largely abandoned seem capable of filling this need. The infrastructure of the present order is essential to understanding contemporary world politics. At present, in matters political, men are disposed to transfer their most important moral impulses to the state. "The morality that peoples practice in their mutual relations is in large measure the product of their historical partitioning. They are refractory to a higher morality only because their sentiments, like their interests, continue to gravitate exclusively about the units which are today the Nation-States. These, though theoretically subordinate to the higher unity, are in fact real and almost absolute centers of moral cohesion. . . . 'Sacred egoism,' the fascist formula, was only the blustering expression of a certain collective morality which makes the national good the supreme good and civil duty the absolute duty." "Merely to invoke the idea of an international community, as is the habit, is immediately to move into a vicious circle, for it is to postulate in men, shut in their national compartments, something they still largely lack, namely the community spirit, the deliberate adherence to supranational values." The criticism Judge de Visscher levels against much of twentieth-century international law is that

[1] All quotations from Judge Charles de Visscher are drawn from *Theory and Reality in Public International Law,* translated from the French by P. E. Corbett (Princeton: Princeton University Press, 1957).

"it exaggerated the specificity of international law, separating it off from the moral, social and political data which form its sphere of application and condition its effectiveness." No social or legal reform that would succeed can ignore the moral infrastructure. The failure of ventures like collective security, the outlawry of war, and sweeping appeals to worldwide public opinion are all examples of thinking that suffers from the illusion that moral foundations are unimportant.

Third, Judge de Visscher calls for a transvaluation of the present structure in terms of a drastic change in the modern conception of the state and its power. Whether his "positive solution" will suffer the shipwreck to which others have fallen prey remains to be seen. He maintains that the ends of the state must be subordinated to those of the human person. The human end of politics from a purely formal point of view "may be defined as the pursuit of the common good, understood as that which in a community should ensure the good of each in the good of the collectivity." Whenever the notion of the common good is no longer harnessed to human ends, there sets in a fatal deterioration in the ends of power. These human ends have been dealt with somewhat naïvely and impatiently in declarations by the United Nations in the proposed Covenant of Human Rights. But De Visscher concludes:

It is the fate of any idea of a highly spiritual character to be exposed to some distortion when it is introduced into a new environment. . . . [Yet] the bond that is being established beyond any shadow of doubt between the rights of man on the one hand, and the maintenance of peace and respect for law on the other, constitutes the first assertion by the international organization of a great moral and civilizing principle. A . . . functional conception of power here joins hands with Christian doctrine, making human values—the only values that can command universal acceptance—the ultimate point of convergence of peace and law. We must neither count upon its immediate efficacy, nor reject the hopes that it awakens.

A second thinker whose writings illuminate the problem before us is Reinhold Niebuhr—Protestant theologian, political philosopher, and precursor of the realist school of thought in international politics. George F. Kennan has called him "the father of all of us." As early as 1932 Professor Niebuhr in *Moral Man and Immoral Society* was grappling with the stubborn issues of international politics, and the publication of his monumental *The Structure of Nations and Empires* promises to add the capstone to his theorizing in this treacherous and uncertain field. Professor John H. Hallowell has written of his approach: "Dr. Niebuhr's analyses make the impact they do upon modern minds because they 'ring true'. . . . We are attracted to his analysis because it confirms what history and our personal experience confirms. He makes explicit what we have been unable before to articulate but what we have felt to be true." The writings of this remarkable theologian over a period of more than forty years come to more than fifteen hundred articles and book reviews and sixteen major volumes. In a field he calls his avocation, a torrent of comment on contemporary social and political problems has issued forth, prompted at least partly by the pressure of world events. He notes that before World War I he was "a young man trying to be an optimist without falling into sentimentality." When the war ended and the full tragedy had been revealed he "had become a realist trying to save himself from cynicism."

Niebuhr's starting point is that of philosopher-theologian rather than international lawyer. International society as we know it today rests fundamentally on man as history reveals him through the ages. The practice of rooting political and legal theory in political institutions and processes rather than probing deeper to the level of human nature has been a peculiar affliction of international law and relations theory. Niebuhr, by contrast, explicitly assumes that an understanding of political phenomena, whether international or domestic, is inseparable from a clear picture of human nature. The Gifford Lectures, begun at the University of Edinburgh in the spring of 1939 as warclouds hovered over Europe and completed in the autumn as the threat became a dreadful reality, represent their author's most systematic attempt to demonstrate the need for and broad outlines of a realistic theory of human nature. The lectures begin: "Man has always been his most vexing problem. How shall he think of himself?" [2] Any affirmation he makes involves him in contradictions. If he stresses man's unique and rational qualities, then man's greed, lust for power, and brute nature betray him. If he holds that men everywhere are the product of nature and unable to rise above circumstances, he tells us nothing of man the creature who dreams of God and of making himself God and of man whose sympathy knows no bounds. If he believes man is essentially good and attributes all evil to concrete historical and social causes, he merely begs the question, for these causes are revealed, on closer scrutiny, to be the consequences of the evil inherent in man. If he finds man bereft of all virtue, his capacity for reaching such a judgment refutes the terms of his judgment. Such baffling paradoxes of human self-knowledge point up the vexing problem of doing justice at one and the same time to the uniqueness of man and to his affinities with nature. Only a theory inspired by a knowledge of both qualities can be adequate. "The obvious fact is that man is a child of nature, subject to its vicissitudes, compelled by its necessities, driven by its impulses, and confined within the brevity of the years which nature permits its varied organic form, allowing them some, but not too much, latitude. The other less obvious fact is that man is a spirit who stands outside of nature, life, himself, his reason and the world." [3] Modern views of man which stress exclusively his dignity or his misery are fatuous and

[2] Reinhold Niebuhr, *The Nature and Destiny of Man*, Vol. I: *Human Nature* (New York: Charles Scribner's Sons, 1945), p. 1.
    [3] *Ibid.*, p. 3.

irrelevant chiefly because they fail to understand the dualism
of man's nature.

The paradox of man's existence arises from the fact that he
is suspended perilously between freedom and finiteness, spirit
and nature. Through spirit he is enabled to survey the whole,
but in so doing he is betrayed into imagining himself the
whole. While enabled through freedom to use the forces
and processes of nature creatively, he comes to ignore his own
creatureliness. His ambiguous and contradictory position at
the juncture of freedom and finiteness produces in him a condition of anxiety which is fundamental to understanding
political behavior.

For our purposes, the most important observable expression of human anxiety is politically in the will-to-power. Man
shares with animals their natural appetites and desires and
the impulse for survival. Yet being both nature and spirit,
his requirements are qualitatively heightened; they are raised
irretrievably to the level of spirit, where they become limit-
less and insatiable. "Man being more than a natural creature,
is not interested merely in physical survival but in prestige
and social approval. Having the intelligence to anticipate the
perils in which he stands in nature and history, he invariably
seeks to gain security against these perils by enhancing his
power, individually and collectively." [4] To overcome social
anxiety, man seeks power over his fellows endeavoring to
subduc their wills to his lest they come to dominate him. The
struggle for political power is merely an example of the
rivalry which goes on at every level of human life.

The human predicament, however, has its roots primarily
in what may be called the security-power dilemma. Weak
men and nations assume that if they had more power they
would be more secure. Yet "The more power an individual
and nation has, the more of its life impinges upon other life

---

[4] Reinhold Niebuhr, *The Children of Light and the Children of Darkness*,
(New York: Charles Scribner's Sons, 1944), p. 20.

and the more wisdom is required to bring it into some decent harmony with other life." [5] Niebuhr notes the ferocity and intensity of the struggle among groups, when compared to the rivalry of individuals, stemming from the tendency of collectivities like the nation to express both the virtue and selfishness of their members. One consequence of modern mass society has been to thwart the attainment of personal security and the satisfaction of basic human aspirations, especially for particular groups. Frustrated individuals strive to fulfil themselves vicariously by projecting their ego to the level of the national ego. In mass society collective attainments offer possibilities of self-realization and self-aggrandizement which individual pretensions no longer serve. At the same time, appeals are made to the loyalty, self-sacrifice, and devotion of individuals in the group. In this way, social unity is built on the virtuous as well as the selfish side of man's nature; the twin elements of collective strength become self-sacrificial loyalty and frustrated aggressions. From this it follows that politics is the more contentious and ruthless because of the unselfish loyalty of the members of groups, which become laws unto themselves unrestrained by their obedient and worshipful followers. Group pride is in fact the corruption of individual loyalty and group consciousness; contempt for another group is the pathetic form which respect of our own frequently takes. The tender emotions which bind the family together sometimes are expressed in indifference for the welfare of other families. In international society a nation made up of men of the greatest religious good will would be less than loving toward other nations, for its virtue would be channeled into loyalty to itself, thus increasing that nation's selfishness. The consequence for Niebuhr's political theory is his conclusion that "society . . . merely cumulates the egoism of individuals and transmutes their individual altruism into collective egoism so that the

[5] *Christianity and Society*, XI, No. 3 (Spring 1945), 7–8.

egoism of the group has a double force. For this reason no group acts from purely unselfish or even mutual intent and politics is therefore bound to be a contest of power." [6]

Niebuhr is inclined to say that the concept of national interest is central to the study of world politics. He observes that "Nations are, on the whole, not generous. A wise self-interest is usually the limit of their moral achievements . . ." [7] The demands of self-interest and national self-protection inspire actions that appear to override all accepted moral impulses. For example, the decision to build the hydrogen bomb gave offense to many sincere people. However, Niebuhr more than once has cautioned humanitarian critics of American foreign policy against assuming that the limits of choice for a nation are broader than they are. Of the bomb he observed in 1950: "No nation will fail to take even the most hazardous adventure into the future, if the alternative of not taking the step means the risk of being subjugated." [8] "Every nation is guided by self-interest and does not support values which transcend its life, if the defense of these values imperils its existence. A statesman who sought to follow such a course would be accused of treason." [9] "No nation ever supports values which transcend its life if they are diametrically opposed to the preservation of its life." [10] Even in considering the Marshall Plan, Niebuhr declared: "As is always the case in international relations, what is called for is not an act of benevolence but of wise self-interest." [11]

This conception of the primacy of national interest broadly conceived has not been popularly acceptable or widely congenial in our liberal democratic age. Idealists and adherents of scientific humanism have maintained that concern for the

[6] Reinhold Niebuhr, "Human Nature and Social Change," *Christian Century*, L (1953), 363.
[7] *Christianity and Crisis*, IX, 21 (Dec. 12, 1949), 162.
[8] *Ibid.*, X, No. 2 (Feb. 20, 1950), 10.
[9] *Radical Religion*, IV, No. 3 (Summer 1939), 7.
[10] *Ibid.*, IV, No. 4 (Autumn 1939), 2.
[11] *Christianity and Society*, XII, No. 4 (Autumn 1947), 3.

safety, integrity, and preservation of the nation-state belonged to an older authoritarian age. Some observers have looked to international organization as one substitute for the national interest. Its more fervent and ebullient protagonists have implored others to abandon selfish national and parochial attachments for more universal loyalties. In contrast, Niebuhr has conceived of international organization as essentially another framework within which historic and emergent national purposes might be pursued and adjusted. For him it has never symbolized the demise of national interests.

Another popular approach to the displacement of the national interest derives from the view that unresolved conflicts among nations would quickly be resolved once taken out of the hands of statesmen and assigned to men of culture or science or education. Niebuhr has associated this view with UNESCO. He has questioned the "belief that the difficulties which statesmen face in guiding their nations are due, not so much to their responsible relation to their several nations, as to their intellectual inferiority in comparison with cultural leaders. This misses the whole point in the encounter of nations with each other. Such an encounter is a power-political one, in which statesmen distinguish themselves from philosophers and scientists, not by their smaller degree of intelligence but by their higher degree of responsibility to their respective communities." [12] Any responsible leader must look first to his nation's security.

Sectarian Christianity and modernist religion in particular have sometimes promised release from the hard demands of the national interest through a religious renaissance whereby partial loyalties would be swallowed up in universal faith. In February 1941 Niebuhr founded his journal, *Christianity and Crisis,* with the primary goal of re-examining the Protestant and secular solutions to the complex problems of the political and economic order. But in contrast to those modern

[12] *Christianity and Crisis,* IX, No. 17 (Oct. 17, 1949), 132.

Christians who seek at almost every point to commend their faith as the source of the qualities and discipline required to save the world from disaster, Niebuhr as Christian has remained self-critical, judicious, and reserved. For example, some Christian leaders have maintained in opposition to their secular critics that democracy is the product of the spiritual resources of religious faith. In their view, democracy is the direct outgrowth of Christian faith. However, this sweeping proposition is unacceptable to Niebuhr since, as a matter of history, *both* Christian and secular forces were involved in establishing the political institutions of democracy. Moreover, there are traditional non-democratic Christian cultures to the right of free societies which prove that the Christian faith does not inevitably yield democratic fruits. A fairer appraisal leads to the conclusion that free societies are a fortunate product of the confluence of Christian and secular forces. More specifically in this country, Christianity and Judaism provide a view of man incompatible with his subordination to any political system, while secular and some forms of religious thought combine to assure critical judgments of human ends and ambitions, social forces and political powers, in order that the false idolatries of modern tyrannies may be avoided. Christianity provides insights through which the chances for democracy are improved, as with the Christian concept of human dignity, making all efforts to fit man into any political program, even in the name of social engineering, morally ambiguous or offensive. Moreover, individual freedom is encouraged by the assumption of a source of authority from which the individual can defy the authorities of this world. ("We must obey God rather than Man.") The Biblical insistence that the same radical freedom which makes man creative also makes him potentially dangerous and destructive leads to the requirements of restraints, balance of power, and equilibrium of social forces upon which effective democracy in action generally rests.

Beyond this, however, there is another part of the story involving the hazards of the relationship between Christianity and democracy and the positive contributions of secular thought. On the one hand, there are grave historical and psychological perils in associating ultimate religious truths with immediate and proximate causes. "Christians cannot deny that the religious theory of divine right of kings has been a powerful force in traditional societies; nor must they obscure the fact that even a true religion frequently generates false identifications of some human interest with God's will." [13] On the other hand, the ascribing of secular content to the non-sacred objects and ends of society has endowed a multitude of lesser activities with a practical moral respectability and at the same time discouraged the premature sanctities in which both traditional societies and modern collectivism abound. It should be noted that an explicit secularism disavowing reverence for the ultimate may itself generate false idolatries, such as the worship of efficiency, or a powerful leader, or the self-sufficient individual. Compared with the noxious idolatries of modern secular totalitarianism, however, they are comparatively harmless, but they prove that an explicit denial of the ultimate may be the basis for a secular religion with excessive pretensions and sanctities of its own.

On the international scene religion can be the means of inspiring patience, humility, and forebearance among states; but the evidence of its transforming qualities are more modest than is frequently claimed. We have recently heard repeatedly from high places renewed requests for greater emphasis on spiritual values as contrasted with material or national interest. Spiritual values are considered abstractly as if they were something that could be added or subtracted from what a nation already had. Our problems, however, involve persistent questions like freedom and order or peace and power, and it can be said that "we do not solve them

[13] *Ibid.*, XII, No. 3 (March 2, 1953), 20.

simply by devotion to abstractly conceived spiritual values." [14]
Moreover, these problems are nicely symbolized by the fact
that the atomic weapons which give us an immediate security
by deterring the aggressor can easily become the means of
civilization's material and moral destruction. "A Christian
faith which declares that all of these horrible ambiguities
would not exist if only we loved each other, is on exactly the
same level as a secular idealism which insists that we could
easily escape our predicament if only we organized a world
government." [15] One Christian moralist recently observed
that if Christians were only sufficiently unselfish to be willing
to sacrifice "their" civilization as faith has prepared them to
sacrifice "their" life we would quickly solve the problem of
war. It is fair to ask how an individual responsible for the
interests of his group is to justify the sacrifice of interests
other than his own. Moreover, "in such terms, Christian
unselfishness requires that we capitulate to tyranny because
democracy happens to be 'ours' and tyranny is 'theirs.' Thus
disloyalty and irresponsibility toward the treasures of an
historic civilization become equated with Christian love." [16]
In Niebuhr's opinion, such viewpoints deserve the name of
soft utopianism.

But modernist religion is as often irrelevant because it
fosters a hard utopianism. A hard utopianism is best char-
acterized by a crusading moralistic approach, wherein every
moral scruple is subject to suppression because a nation assumes it is fighting for God and a Christian civilization
against atheism. It is ironic that we should so endlessly appeal
to the moral supremacy of our cause at the moment when
Communism, as distinct from Fascism, is claiming to embody
the absolute objective moral law. On reflection we can observe that Communists are so evil primarily because they are

[14] Reinhold Niebuhr, "The Cultural Crisis of Our Age," *Harvard Business
Review*, XXXII, No. 1 (Jan.–Feb. 1954), 34.
[15] *Christianity and Crisis*, XL, No. 1 (Feb. 5, 1951), 3.
[16] *Ibid.*

idolators—not atheists—who in their fierce moral idealism are willing to sacrifice every decency and scruple to one wholly illusory value: the classless society. Democracies run a somewhat similar risk by claiming too much for their moral cause whether by design or through ignorance of its partial and fragmentary character. In describing the problems of postwar American foreign policy, especially in maintaining allies, Niebuhr explains: "Our difficulty is significantly that we claim moral superiority over them too easily, not recognizing that each man and nation erects a pyramid of moral preferences on the basis of a minimum moral law." [17] Because of the pluralistic character of national values, this law is most universal when it states obligations in minimum and negative terms such as "Thou shalt not steal."

But the moral issue in international relations even with these restrictions remains the fundamental problem. If in international organization, men of culture and modern religion are unsuccessful in supplying the instruments by which national interest can be transcended, Niebuhr is nevertheless persuaded that men and states cannot follow their interest without claiming to do so in obedience to some general scheme of values. Two very grave moral and practical questions have continued to trouble him and have led him to make a series of distinctions regarding the national interest. First, he has asked whether a consistent emphasis upon the national interest is not as self-defeating in national life as it is in individual life. Or put in other terms, does not a nation concerned too much with its own interests define those interests so narrowly and so immediately (as, for instance, in terms of military security) that the interests and securities, which depend upon common devotion to principles of justice and upon established mutualities in a community of nations, are sacrificed? Secondly, nations, which insist on the

[17] Reinhold Niebuhr, "Christianity and the Moral Law," *The Christian Century*, LXX, No. 48 (Dec. 2, 1953), 1386.

one hand that they cannot act beyond their interest, claim, as soon as they act, that they have acted not out of self-interest but in obedience to higher objectives like "civilization" or "justice." Applied to the conduct of contemporary American foreign relations, we claim more for the benevolence of our policies than they deserve and arouse the resentment of peoples already inclined to envy our power and wealth. Thus national interest is imperiled at one time by the hazard of moral cynicism and at another time by moral pretension and hypocrisy. In his earlier writings on the subject Niebuhr has dealt with the first of these questions and more recently with the second. In the evolution of his thinking, moreover, he has come to view them as parts of a single problem. The problem involves our continued ambivalence toward the moral issue, claiming at one moment that nations have no obligations beyond their interests and at the next moment that they are engaged in a high moral crusade without regard for interests.

Moral cynicism arises from the identification of the brutal facts with the normative aspects of international politics. Interest which is the lowest common denominator of political behavior is made the highest practical standard. Yet it is of course obvious that the ultimate norms of religion are almost never the effective ethical standards of politics—a realm generally marked by some form of coercion, force, or resistance.

Pacifists and perfectionists who undertake to translate the law of love of the Kingdom of God directly into the language of politics provide at best a protest and at worst a wholly unrealistic and harmful alternative to a more cynical approach. They try to make a success story out of the story of the Cross. There is one form of pacifism, pragmatic in character, which accepts the world as it is with interest set against interest and seeks through political imagination and intelligence to adjust, harmonize, and mitigate the conflict on the assumption that overt violence is a great social evil. For the most part, however, the purest standards of love and generosity are not directly relevant to the life of nations. But neither are they wholly irrelevant as final norms, for while love is impossible in that it is never fully realizable in history, it never loses its significance as an ultimate moral norm. It inspires and makes possible ethical conduct at a more proximate level and provides a standard against which social ethics may be evaluated and judged.

If the standard of love is to be made useful and relevant, however, it must be translated into relative and proximate terms more appropriate to the realities of politics. For Niebuhr justice satisfies this demand as the most significant approximation of the ideal of love in politics. But justice involving the compromise of love with the darker elements of politics is also its contradiction. It should be explained that Niebuhr in his analysis of the international scene proceeds simultaneously at two levels. He constructs a rational theory of the behavior of states based on the primacy of their interests, and here he travels the same road as other contemporary realists. "Beyond national interest," however, he is concerned to establish a normative theory in order to avert what he has called the abyss of moral cynicism inherent in a merely rational theory. In this he provides guideposts both for those who are persuaded by his approach and for those who seek another way.

Several thousands of miles and the intellectual and political distance between a philosopher and a statesman separate Professor Niebuhr and the great British leader Winston S. Churchill. Yet significantly enough both discover foundations for their theories in human nature. Facing the crisis of our age, Churchill can write: "Man at this moment of his history has emerged in greater supremacy over the forces of nature than has ever been dreamed of before. He has it in his power to solve quite easily the problems of material existence. He has conquered the wild beasts, and he has even conquered the insects and the microbes. There lies before him if he wishes, a golden age of peace and progress. All is in his hand. He has only to conquer his last and worst enemy—himself." Neither law nor institutions but man is fundamental to Mr. Churchill. Therefore, the student may with reason consider him alongside jurists and philosophers and affirm with C. S. Forester that: "In millennia to come, his work will be studied as we now study Thucydides and Tacitus. . . ." Despite this, Churchill himself is unwilling to consider his volumes on *The Second World War* as true history, speaking of them rather as his "contribution." Yet embedded in them and in his political acts and public and private justifications is a more or less explicit conception of international life that bears directly on our subject.

Churchill plainly has never shared the widespread belief that a brave new world is in process of unfolding. His world is one which is changing but not one where old truths can be set aside. He has been particularly impatient when contemporary prophets have asserted that science and man's prospect of moral and rational perfection would transform international society. Science, he believes, is for men a neutral and amoral force, while the great issues are intellectual, moral, and political. Whereas the consequences of applying science to the exploitation of natural resources are automatic and certain, the results which flow from plans and policies in the social order are always beclouded, ambiguous, and uncertain. In politics he finds no substitute for political judgment. While physical resources and scientific data can be accumulated and stored, political wisdom can never be stockpiled in any comparable way. The essence of politics is such that Mr. Churchill is loath to entrust its responsibilities to scientific experts or administrative specialists. Half mockingly, he notes: "On many occasions in the past we have seen attempts to rule the world by experts of one kind or another. There have been the theocratic, the military and the aristocratic and it is now suggested that we should have scientistic—not scientific—governments." [18] He harks back to Gladstone, who "said many years ago that it ought to be part of a man's religion to see that his country is well governed. Knowledge of the past is the only foundation we have from which to peer into and measure the future. Expert knowledge, however indispensable, is no subtitute for a generous and comprehending outlook upon the human story with all its sadness and with all its unquenchable hope." [19]

Science and democracy, which are frequently conceived of as the twin sources through which the painful divisions and rivalries in society can be relieved, must in practice be held partly accountable for the intensification of conflict. Mass societies unleash powerful social forces that deny a place to that small body of well-trained professionals whose skill, to paraphrase Mr. Churchill, gives a state that beautiful intricacy of diplomatic and military maneuver so essential to its security. Those qualities of humanity and chivalry which were the glory of a less troubled Europe are threatened and will probably be destroyed. They are qualities which the humanities and not the sciences best supply, and without them man can scarcely achieve full stewardship of the weapons and secrets he has wrested from nature. The ancients considered the paramount task of the university inculcating clear thinking on the themes of government. Science can offer no alternative to this. Rather it places in jeopardy the intrinsic qualities of individualism by which humanity has traditionally advanced. Indeed there are those who would replace society itself by science. As a principal speaker at the commemoration of the founding of a great scientific institution of learning, Massachusetts Institute of Technology, Britain's wartime leader observed:

[18] *Time*, Nov. 19, 1945, p. 29.
[19] Quoted by Mr. Churchill in a speech at the University of Miami, Feb. 26, 1946; printed in *The Sinews of Peace* (a collection of wartime speeches) (Boston: Houghton Miffllin, 1949), p. 92.

In his introductory address, Dr. Burchard, the Dean of Humanities, spoke with awe of "an approaching scientific ability to control men's thoughts with precision." I shall be very content if my task in this world is done before that happens. Laws just or unjust may govern men's actions. Tyrannies may restrain or regulate their minds with falsehood and deny them truth for many generations of time.

But the soul of man thus held in a trance or frozen in a long night can be awakened by a spark coming from God knows where and in a moment the whole structure of lies and oppression is on trial for its life. . . . Science no doubt could if sufficiently perverted exterminate us all; but it is not in the power of material forces in any period which the youngest here tonight need take into practical account, to alter the main elements in human nature or restrict the infinite variety of forms in which the soul and genius of the human race can and will express itself.[20]

If we turn to the positive foundations of Mr. Churchill's philosophy, we find his opposition to the uncritical admiration of everything scientific rooted fundamentally in his comprehension of the essential character of politics. Present-day efforts to reduce all politics to an exact science in which every political development can be foreseen and predicted err by neglecting three basic characteristics of politics. Mr. Churchill believes that whatever the goals and extrinsic character of politics, its intrinsic qualities especially on the international scene are everywhere the same. In the first place, international politics, while not identical with force, supplies a rational alternative, as well as a basic deterrent, to force. It is of course true and even axiomatic that politics is a struggle for power. Some have interpreted this to mean that politics is war by proxy of military forces. But force or military strength and its use are only incidents. The problems of politics are endless. Force and warfare are those expressions of power in which the capacity of individuals and nations are tested and decided. But the problems of politics endure

[20] *New York Times,* April 1, 1949, p. 10.

and know of no decisive solutions. In human affairs, the best we can hope for is to discover some kind of relatively stable equilibrium of power which through insight and steadiness may be wisely adapted in the interests of peace. Force is so ambiguous as a determinant of political power because it is always relative to somebody else's potential means of force. And the baffling and difficult prospect of comparing the elements of strength makes politics something other than an exact science. Mr. Churchill reflected on these more subtle aspects of politics when he wrote as late as 1951: "It is said that we are getting stronger, but to get stronger does not necessarily mean that we are getting safer. It is only when we are strong enough that safety is achieved; and the period of the most acute danger might well arise just before we were strong enough." [21]

Therefore, the capacity to use force effectively is decisive as an element of political power only if that capacity is as significant in relative terms as it is in itself. That is, nations whose power is sufficient to warn any ambitious or aggressive friend or foe that a test of military strength would be more expensive in lives and resources than other alternatives can encourage the use of a peaceful alternative to force. For politics presumes that through checks and balances individuals and groups, however ambitious, will generally refrain from a use of violence if in so doing they would jeopardize their own self-interests. Indeed recent foreign policy in the West is logical and intelligible only to the degree that this principle is comprehended. The program we are supporting to deter the Russians derives from this principle and the fate of our nation is intimately bound up in its validity. Many Americans, and indeed many Europeans, under the spell of the liberal illusion about power politics have judged the rearmament program in Europe and this country in ex-

[21] *Parliamentary Debates*, Vol. 487, May 10, 1951, p. 2161.

clusively military terms. For example, we have often been told that the rearmament program could be justified because at a certain date in the foreseeable future we would be able to turn back the Russians at some line or other, or, conversely, that it should be rejected because the chances of success or a military victory at any time in the foreseeable future did not exist. Yet there is an alternative to both these propositions and it is the one on which responsible leaders base their thinking. In a word, it is the conception that a deterrent to Russian expansion can be created which will invite them to seek their objectives through means other than military expansion. However, this concept remains essentially meaningless unless the inseparable relationship of force and politics to their source in rivalries and struggles for power is fully comprehended. In general, even for aggrandizing states politics will be chosen as a means to the end of domination and control if there are sufficient deterrents to the use of force to make the peaceful the more rational alternative: "I have always held the view that the maintenance of peace depends upon the accumulation of deterrents against aggression." [22] In these terms peace takes on a special light for men like Churchill who must proclaim as he did in 1936: "I am looking for peace. I am looking for a way to stop war, but you will not stop it by pious sentiments and appeals. You will only stop it by making practical arrangements. . . ." [23] These practical steps are not simply the use or threat of force. Nor are they merely the profession of good and peaceful intentions. They are steps which aim at erecting an edifice of political power. At this moment in history such a goal presumes as one of its pillars the growth of Anglo-American unity. "Neither the sure prevention of war, nor the continuous rise of world organization will be gained

[22] *Parliamentary Debates*, Vol. 339, Oct. 5, 1938, p. 362.
[23] *Parliamentary Debates*, Vol. 310, March 26, 1936, pp. 1529–1530.

without what I have called the fraternal association of the English-speaking peoples." [24] This means a special relationship between the British Commonwealth and Empire and the United States. It also includes the emergent power of Western Europe without dogmatic and inflexible ideological tests. But in the present and for the foreseeable future the best deterrent remains the power of the United States. For "We must be under no delusion that it is not American armed force which preserves the peace of the world at the moment." [25]

With these proposals, we are in the presence of little that is new or unusual from a concrete or specific point of view. The steps and measures that Mr. Churchill is urging have been recommended by others as well. It is the over-all theory undergirding his recommendations which is novel at this time or rather which is often concealed or obscured and therefore overlooked. For it is precisely an understanding of the nature of politics which presents the most serious theoretical and practical difficulty for many contemporary analysts. The prevailing errors, on the one hand, of disregarding the intimate relationship of politics and force or, conversely, the mistakes of equating the two are avoided in Mr. Churchill's approach. For to him it is axiomatic that they are merely alternate expressions of the unceasing struggle for power among nations. It is because politics is so intimately related to force, at least internationally, that the effective balancing of power within this sphere can postpone or prevent perilous resorts to force.

The second aspect of politics of which Mr. Churchill in his political actions reminds us is its provisional and prudential character. The tactics of politics are immediate and tentative. The measures that nations take can be identified with more general causes than their own interests only at grave

[24] *New York Times*, March 6, 1946, p. 4.
[25] *The Times* (London), April 22, 1948, p. 6.

risk of failure, hypocrisy, and vacillation. For those who espouse in lectures and speech broad and lofty humanitarian objectives, it is unfortunately true that nations in their policies pursue programs of this order only when their own national interests are not jeopardized thereby. Symbolic of the practical aspects of politics is Mr. Churchill's approach to the problem of Spain. On September 19, 1945, when the immediate and overwhelming threat from the east was not yet everywhere apparent, he bluntly rejected General Franco's requests: "It is out of the question for the British Government to support Spanish aspirations in future peace settlements, nor do I think it likely that Spain will be invited to join a future world organisation." [26] By May 12, 1949, however, the changing conditions of international politics and the increasing menace of Russian imperialism having become apparent, he felt called upon to say: "The absence of Spain from the Atlantic Pact involves, of course, a serious gap in the strategic arrangements for Western Europe. I was glad to hear . . . [the favorable expression for] the return of ambassadors. I do not ask more than that at the present time." [27]

If it were not for the practical requirements of politics, these changes of policy in emphasis if not in substance could be properly denounced as blatant inconsistencies. But since it is politics we are considering in which actions must be provisional and attuned to changing circumstances, adaptation in the interest of the objectives of states becomes essential. Since politics are pre-eminently practical and provisional, we must look for consistency not in each concrete political action of the nation but in the more general principle which inspires the conduct of foreign policy. We can discover this principle in the broad concept of the national interest. It is here in what is general to all international action and not in

[26] *New York Times*, Sept. 19, 1945, p. 18.
[27] *Parliamentary Debates*, Vol. 464, May 12, 1949, p. 2027.

the particular and specific undertakings of a state that consistency can be found. For the steps nations take in the conduct of policy are by the nature of contemporary international politics limited and prudential in character. Only as they contribute to security and survival are these measures justified and clarified.

A third characteristic of politics must be noted which differentiates it most vividly from other spheres with which it is frequently confused and confounded. Politics is qualitatively different from philosophy. Its guides are relative and the sole absolutes it knows are those which can be associated with successful political action. One of these principles is the rule of the balance of power. Another is the iron rule that compromise, while impossible on matters of principle, is practical and essential for a whole range of issues comprising political interests. It is the virtue of political action that the actor in politics remains free to negotiate and explore so long as he is guided by a sense of his nation's true interests.

The realm of politics is one in which the participants must choose from alternatives made legitimate not by abstract principles but by their relation to the viability of the nation at any given time. It may be mandatory that certain lines of action be followed on particular occasions and others pursued under other conditions. But there are no absolute principles which can provide ready-made answers to these painful choices. It is even conceivable to this arch-British-patriot that through novel arrangements some way would be found to relate the British, despite their historic policy of freedom of action in Europe, to some proposed plan for Western European Union. If the realm of politics is looked at in absolute terms with respect to the forms in which the traditional interests of nations have expressed themselves, Mr. Churchill's next proposition must be interpreted as some form of political stratagem. But if we assume that the relative character of political action establishes a wide range and variety of practical measures, then what he declared on June 27, 1950, assumes its own type of political wisdom: "Although a hard-and-fast concrete federal constitution for Europe is not within the scope of practical affairs, we should help, sponsor and aid in every possible way the movement towards European unity. We should seek steadfastly for means to become intimately associated with it." [28]

Finally it is no exaggeration to say that the Western World has faced no more bewildering and compelling problem than the question of the moral evaluation of foreign policy. In part the problem has been so bewildering because most observers have tended either to exaggerate or underestimate the influence in practice of moral principles. The insistent and compelling character of the problem, moreover, is revealed by the fact that Western civilization has suffered from an uneasy conscience about the nature of politics. It is true that in the English-speaking world in particular, questions of political morality have been debated and decided only when required by contemporary events. Yet this approach, which in practice has made for an avoidance of generalized propositions about international morality, has never deterred Western man from deciding upon the morality or amorality of issues and policies presented within the narrow confines of concrete political situations. It has been as "cases" in political morality that these issues have been debated before the bar of public opinion and in theory, at least, been judged and decided according to the right reason of majority rule. The question of international morality has been conceived of not in any comprehensive systematic framework but in terms of the practical merits of specific issues.

The most simple and appealing approach to the moral aspects of foreign policy has been the one growing out of the distinction between the moralist and the political realist. In

[28] *Parliamentary Debates,* Vol. 476, June 27, 1950, p. 2157.

our American negotiations with other nations it is frequently said that we cherish certain uncompromisable principles on which we can never make concessions. Other countries, it has been said, are often devoid of such principles in
their political practice. We are resolved to pursue only the
general international good; other nations are cynically concerned about their own interests. According to this outlook
if strictly observed, our negotiations would be inherently
affected both in the width and depth of discussions by the
permanent limitation that principles must be a part of any
bargain which could be consummated. Realism, on the contrary, contends that principles, while as a rule the objects of
negotiation, need not necessarily be an intrinsic part of the
agreement itself. In so far as the end of the discussions is
appropriate, the means to the end become justifiable. Indeed
in practice the end, which in foreign policy is the security
and power of the nation, justifies almost any means that may
be taken for its attainment. When we consider this problem
in greater detail, however, we shall see that this puts the
problem too crudely and simply.

In order to discover where Mr. Churchill takes his stand
with respect to these two alternatives we may turn at this
point to examine his words and actions. Since man is by
nature an ethical being who must conceive of the things that
he does in their essential moral setting, it is not surprising
that Mr. Churchill's philosophy should be richly endowed
with ethical lessons and meaning. The ethics of his philosophy, however, are cast in terms which depart from those
of the popularly supported moral crusades. His ethics are not
the simple ethics of unambiguous progress, social reform, or
general world betterment. Instead his conception of political
morality has been hammered and shaped by the stern blows
of practical experience. His professions of faith in the mid-
twentieth century are profoundly the outgrowth of disap-
pointment and disillusionment with the practical reality of

other ideals which he championed at the turn of the century. As a young man in the military service, he looked with anguish and dismay at the sufferings and oppression of Indians, South Africans, and Asians. His youthful experiences left imprinted on his conscience the need for tolerance and greater equality. He said at the time that it was imperative that the military victories of British troops in these areas should be followed by sincere efforts to help the fallen peoples to rise. And as he found tolerance and humanitarianism proper expressions of an innate morality, he discovered in his own private form of pacifism a worthy companion to these convictions. Having tasted military honor in the thick of the most primitive military conflicts, he espoused the holy cause of pacifism as a general philosophy to guide him in his actions. His biographer reports that he described the Army Reform of February 13, 1903, as "The Great English Fraud." He insisted that expenditures for the army were excessive and extravagant and that the professional soldier was a costly and artificial luxury. It was an unwarranted and unnecessary outlay to provide for more than the bare minimum of military personnel, who were inevitably withdrawn from the nation's industrial and family life at so great a price. He opposed the Broderick military program, which would have provided for an army of 150,000 English soldiers organized in army corps based on the German model. The precarious eminence of England, whose crowded industrial population were balancing perilously on the rim of an artificial economic survival and who were dependent on colonial and foreign markets, made the price of an army too costly, parasitical as it was on the production of the rest of the economy.

When he was a young man of twenty-five, Churchill's moral principles were humanitarianism and pacifism. As these fervent convictions faded away in the crucible of experience, they were not replaced immediately by other equally strong beliefs. Occasionally in this period and up to the time of his exclusion from the coalition cabinet of Lloyd George, Mr. Churchill was referred to with derision as "a man with a duster" who everyone agreed displayed marks of greatness but who lacked the unifying force of a strong character. His effect upon others was to arouse interest and curiosity but rarely to inspire admiration and loyalty. He had the power of gifts but not of a firm and rocklike character. The lightning flashes of his insight pierced the half-gloom of contemporary illusions about political issues. But the beating of a steadfast heart and the force of a powerful and gripping idea were absent and there appeared to be no moral balance-wheel for his intellectual dexterity. He was Saul on the road to Damascus, but until he could find some integrating and empowering idea by which he and his followers could live as well as die, it was unlikely that he would become a Paul on the way to immortality.

History records that after the days of World War I, when these accusations about him were current, Mr. Churchill found his transforming idea. The once dominant theories of progress, social reform, and plans for world betterment became for him issues of an inferior order, each subject to the play of common sense and the passage of time. The real issue became that of preserving the lasting interests of England and of a world order in which such values could survive. His crusade was no longer for general humanitarian objectives. His purpose became rather that of safeguarding the concrete interests of one nation. From humanitarianism, pacifism, and even an indifference to values, Mr. Churchill arrived at the national interest as the shrine in which many of the spirits of political morality reside. Mr. Churchill's transvaluation of values has reached its homeland in the English constitution and in its values. To save these values, he has several times turned from one traditional political party to another. He has been a Conservative, a Liberal, and a "Constitutionalist."

But he would argue that each shift was evoked by the failures of the parties to sustain the spirit of the English system.

There are, however, not one but three dimensions to Mr. Churchill's political morality. The heart or core of his conception is a belief in moral dignity of the national interest. The truths which Washington, Hamilton, and John Quincy Adams declared at the time of our republic's inception are contained in one great tradition of British foreign policy which has an equally respectable ancestry. These truths, in a word, assume that the first duty in a nation's foreign policy must be to safeguard the interests of its citizens and of past and future generations and thereby preserve its moral values. A nation can indulge itself the private virtues of generosity and self-sacrifice only if its own survival is not endangered. If in fact its external acts are restricted because of threats to its security, the nation as a community of men of good will can pursue moral ends and purposes at home and in this way contribute to international order.

A second dimension of Mr. Churchill's conception of international morality is, from one point of view, the other side of the shield of the national interest. It is his idea of the mutuality of national interests. In the United States on January 6, 1952, he said: "We have only to go along together, each doing loyally his best, understanding the other's point of view and the many differences in interest between our countries, and we shall find ourselves safe at the end of the road." [29] History records numerous examples of nations of good will proclaiming their choice of a course of action based on their own enlightened self-interest which was also assumed best for the welfare of all mankind. The illusion of pride counts its victims among all those states who have sought to enlarge their own interests to a universal creed. Indeed the fact that good and bad nations have justified their

[29] *The Times* (London), Jan. 7, 1952, p. 4.

actions on precisely these general grounds is not particularly reassuring. Yet the one thing which saves the idea of the national interest from itself and the overpowering impulses of self-pride is its essential reciprocity. To the extent that nations are in earnest not alone about their own self-interests but in their recognition of similar criteria pursued by others, the national interest as a guide escapes the temptation of concealing its vices in doctrines for universal consumption.

The third dimension of Mr. Churchill's conception of morality comprises those general moral principles, such as opposition to tyranny, which Mr. Churchill has championed from the beginning of his career. We shall consider this dimension again in the discussion of Judaeo-Christian realism. The task of statesmanship at any point in time is to keep these three aspects in balance. What is moral and ethical in any context depends on the calculations made or weighting given the application of the three elements. If the problem of moral imperatives is not made any simpler by virtue of this approach, the outlines of the question are filled out more fully than is often the case. To this the reading of an international jurist, theologian-philosopher, and wise statesman inevitably contribute and their writings furnish a kind of working outline for thinking about the moral ambiguities of present-day international life.

3. *A Concluding Note on the Problem*

The structure and realities of international society then must set the framework for any serious discussion of the moral problem. Somehow the moralist must come to terms with the forces which great minds have confronted and analyzed. In Walter Lippmann's apt phrase: "If the moralist is to deserve a hearing among his fellows, he must set himself this task which is so much humbler than to command and so much more difficult than to exhort: he must seek to anticipate and to supplement the insight of his fellow men into the problems of their adjustment to reality." Neither science alone nor theology nor political philosophy in its perennial concern with the state provides ready-made answers to these dilemmas. The student of international politics, however insufficient he may be and feel, can scarcely leave the problem to others. The moral imperatives that most would agree ought to guide man's conduct in ordinary human relations can hardly be involved as codes of changeless content against which to measure and judge all forms of behavior. It is not so much that absolute moral imperatives are irrelevant, say, for the statesman. Rather men act in a variety of structures which in turn evoke an immense variety of codes of behavior and conduct. Family life, business activities, municipal reform, military combat, and foreign politics each in turn rest on totally different versions of what men are like and how they are expected to act. The code of patriotism, particularly in wartime, assumes one kind of human nature and the commercial code quite another. The moralist may well be tempted to denounce them all and judge them as if he were God. Yet how often we observe a loving father who is also a harsh and demanding boss or an ardent and uncompromising reformer or a soldier who gives no quarter. The central question for the moralist is what he is to think of the endless variety of human situations which through their inner imperatives place peculiar moral burdens on those who act. In wartime, sacrifice for the soldier even of life itself is often required for a dollar a day. But what of the businessman in wartime who far from sacrificing himself expects and receives a handsome profit to produce the means of destruction? Both efforts carried on with energy receive recognition, but neither has validity taken out of its context.

The point of our problem is that modern Western civilization is morally complex, probably far beyond other civilizations. Social systems tend to "give expression to or reflect mores, patterns of culture, implicit assumptions as to the world, deep convictions, unconscious beliefs that make them largely autonomous moral institutions on which instrumental political, economic, religious or other functions are superimposed or from which they evolve." [30] In effect, varied social systems appear to create moralities of their own or at least moralities not identical in immediate application with the pure truths of Judaeo-Christian ethics. This leads a Christian businessman and philanthropist to say, ". . . the Ten Commandments, the Sermon on the Mount, the Golden Rule . . . have so little application to the moral problems of the world of affairs." [31] Or an economist to observe: "A pure personal-relations ethic, of whatever form, can hardly furnish rules for such activities as international trade, or any dealings with people too numerous and remote to have reality for us as individuals. . . ." [32] Or a theologian to argue: "I believe that one of the requirements of the hour is that Christians should cease to present the gospel as a simple panacea for all the world's ills, insisting, for instance, that if only people loved each other, all these evils would disappear. . . . We all know that it is more difficult for collective man, as distinguished from the individual to obey the law of love." He concludes, ". . . we must take the self-interest of nations for granted, and ask the question whether it is possible to achieve standards of justice and accommodation within the limits of this ineradicable self-interest." [33] Or finally prompts the wisest of Western statesmen to confess: "It is baffling to reflect that what men call honour does not correspond always to Christian ethics. . . . An exaggerated code of honour

---

[30] Chester I. Barnard, "Elementary Conditions of Business Morals," *California Management Review*, I, No. 1 (Autumn 1958), 2.

[31] *Ibid.*

[32] Frank H. Knight, "Conflict of Values: Freedom and Justice," in *Goals of Economic Life*, ed. A. Dudley Ward (New York: Harper & Brothers, 1953), pp. 203–230.

[33] This theme runs through the writings of Reinhold Niebuhr, especially such books as *Moral Man and Immoral Society, Christian Realism and Political Problems,* and *Christianity and Power Politics.*

leading only to the performance of utterly vain and unreasonable deeds should not be defended however fine it
might look." [34]

It is probably true that the same strictures which students
of business ethics have levied against a too simple moralism
apply to the writers on international morality. Chester I.
Barnard puts the responsibility for the gap between moralists
and economists in the following words: "The theologians
[speak] . . . of a nomadic and simple agricultural life—of
sheep and lambs, of shepherds—in an industrial age in which
the majority have no experience of rural life. . . . The doctrine of the economists [is] concerned with highly abstract
aggregates of behavior, with . . . assumptions of the maximization of profits as the principle of economic behavior." [35]
How are we to marry, or in any event to relate, the highly
personal ethic of honesty and decency and respect for the
interests of others to the impersonal sphere of concrete business behavior with its imperatives of serving "the good of the
organization" or adherence to correct legal and administrative rules and procedures? Mr. Barnard for his part concludes: "Moral ideals, when expressed in general terms
rather than in action in concrete situations, are necessarily
abstract and attainment may fall far short of the abstract
ideal. This does not mean that failure is evidence of immorality, but that moral achievement is in part dependent
on concrete conditions which vary widely." [36]

All of this points up the profound nature of the moral
problem in international politics. Perhaps the historian
Meinecke has put the problem best: "The laws of morality,
of brotherly love, of sanctity of agreements, are eternal and
inviolable. But the duty of the statesman to care for the
welfare and safety of the state and people entrusted to him

[34] Winston S. Churchill, *The Gathering Storm* (Boston: Houghton Mifflin
Company, 1949), pp. 320–321.
[35] Barnard, *op. cit.*, p. 3.
[36] *Ibid.*, p. 4.

. . . is also sacred and inviolable." He asks, as have other great writers in the Western political tradition, what happens when these two duties conflict.

In the United States liberals and churchmen, internationalists and isolationists, Congressmen and diplomats, journalists and scholars have expressly or by implication tried to answer the question for the better part of the last half-century. Their answers comprise a capsule history of Western thought and, while they resist any convincing system of classification, I find, broadly speaking, four kinds of answers.

Cynicism is one answer, although few consistently maintain that political action can remain permanently bereft of moral content. Hitler presumably set aside all benevolence or loyalty to goals beyond race and state. Stalin's consistent deprecation of the influence of non-Communist ideals and his willingness to sacrifice the human lives of deviationists or kulaks if it served Soviet political purposes was blatantly cynical. The cynic tends to argue, if he justifies himself at all, that politics and ethics are not cut from the same cloth. Politics are means and ethics are ends and, while the means employed may seem evil, good ends can make them good. The simple formula of the end justifying the means has for some brought about resolution of the problem.

Yet for men and for nations, the universal practice is to justify every evil measure by claiming it serves an ethical goal. For Stalin the gross brutality of liquidating the kulaks found justification as an inevitable step in the history-fulfilling Communist design; for Hitler the cremation of so-called inferior races was excused as a necessary hygienic measure if Teutonic superiority were to continue unimpaired. Since nations in the present anarchic world society tend to be repositories of their own morality, the end-means formula has prevailed as an answer to the moral dilemma, for undeniably it is a concealed but essential truth that nations tend to create their own morality.

In its extreme form, however, this development has found nations accepting as ethical whatever redounded to their own material advantage and judging whatever was detrimental to their purposes as immoral and evil. Yet it inheres in the nature of man and politics that statesmen and nations never wholly escape the judgment of elementary ethical standards. The history of politics discloses that no people have completely divorced politics from ethics without, however grudgingly, coming to see that men are required to conform to standards more objective than those of success.

There is another answer—whether it be called hypocrisy or national moralizing. Every person and every nation shares to some extent in this response. For whenever men or nations act, they make larger claims for their morality than can be warranted. If this is deception, it is apparently an almost inevitable form of self-deception since nations no less than individuals must persuade themselves that their deeds are legitimate because consistent with some larger frame of value. The parent never disciplines the child except for its own good. The powerful nation never goes to war except in the interests of peace and justice. The problem about these actions is not that they are all devoid of some residual justice nor that claims of goodness never serve to lift men and groups above the selfish and the mundane. It is rather that we are seldom as moral as we claim to be whether as righteous Jews or Christians or when we speak for the nation as a whole.

A third answer is reformist and apocalyptic in nature. It concedes that at present there may be conflict between the eternal principles of which Meinecke spoke and the imperatives of statecraft. At present men and states pursue selfish and parochial ends but, in Woodrow Wilson's phrase, "national purposes have fallen more and more into the background and the common purpose of enlightened mankind has taken their place." The one point on which liberal and conservative utopians agree is that politics in which there are conflicts of interest is but a passing and ephemeral phase of an earlier inferior aristocratic era.

For the liberal, novel world institutions and world law can transform man. For the conservative, more businessmen with the homely virtues of private life—honesty, simplicity, charm, and geniality—can bridge the gulf between ultimate and political morality. This last philosophy virtually destroys the well-known tension between the private and public spheres or between man *qua* man and man as citizen. It excuses a political leader for failure, irresolution, and imprudence and for ignorance of the demands of politics if only he is honest, well-meaning, and a good fellow.

The reformer cannot believe that in international relations even today situations arise where my nation's justice can mean your nation's injustice; my nation's security and its requirements, your nation's insecurity; and armaments, defense preparations, and alliances can appear as threats to security as viewed through other eyes.

Faced with these realities, the reformist maintains that at present men may indeed pursue a double standard of conduct in their private and public lives. Privately, man is honest and ethical; publicly he covers his acts with a tissue of lies and deception. His virtue in private affairs is seen as the conquest of culture over barbarism, of a rational age over an irrational one. Once in an earlier stage in man's evolution, his private conduct was marred by brutality and violence; but education, a legal order, and free institutions transformed him. In the same way the cultural lag from which nations have suffered in international relations is being erased. The forward march of history is carrying nations from a retarded condition into a new and enlightened era when private standards will become public international rules.

Those who doubt are denounced as foes of progress and

men of little faith. Yet this simple rationalism pays little heed to the depth of the problem. In its zeal it ignores the distance between the two realms. Religious ethics calls self-interest into question. Man must lose himself in order to find himself. As soon as we move to the level of organized communities, the problem of legitimate self-interest arises, for political ethics takes self-interest for granted. A political leader cannot ask his people to sacrifice themselves. His first duty is to preserve the constitution, and he owes allegiance to the safety and well-being of the nation and of its generations yet unborn.

Reinhold Niebuhr has distinguished between moral man and immoral society; and while he has subsequently modified the sharp lines of his dichotomy, he would hold, I believe, to the "hidden truth" which this distinction lays bare. Accordingly, those virtues of gentleness, magnanimity, love, and trust which enrich the dimensions of our family life at its best and are possible in our more intimate communities must be viewed with circumspection, reserve, and uncertainty on the world stage where states through power and force press their claims and counterclaims.

We may as moral beings deplore and denounce the evil portents of a massive armaments program, but who among us, if responsible for the nation's security, would have persisted in meeting Soviet power through compassion and the repudiation of force? Or, who, confronted by the Nazi threat to Western civilization, would have turned aside the proffered alliance of an equally oppressive Communist regime? And today who can say that we should sacrifice as the price of disarmament our anti-missile program just as the prospect of a device capable of tracking and destroying enemy missiles is within sight?

The fourth answer to the problem is the one Meinecke gave. "Every authentic tragedy is a shattering demonstration that moral life cannot be regulated like clockwork and that even the purest strivings for good can be forced into the most painful choices. . . . In relations between states, moreover, clashes between private morality and state interest are plainly inevitable and as old as world history itself."

What sets this outlook apart is its clear recognition of the tension between morality and politics or foreign policy. It alone among the viewpoints of cynicism, hypocrisy, and reformism demands humility. It starts by accepting the persistence of self-interest in all political communities and the impossibility of persuading any community to sacrifice itself. It assumes that the best nations can do is to find the point of concurrence between their interests and purposes and the interests of others as the United States did in Europe but has failed to do up to now in the Middle East. It is reluctant to claim universal validity for national policies and hesitant to proclaim that what is good for me is good for everyone or what my group or nation views as in its interest is in the interest of the whole world. It is as fearful of moral crusades and national self-righteousness as of the outright denial of moral principles.

The names of Churchill, Lincoln, John Quincy Adams, and a handful of great religious leaders epitomize this view. Inescapably it has a place for the tragic element in life, for it leaves for another, better world the utopias and final justice that men and states so often claim for themselves.

Chapter Two

THREE DILEMMAS OF CONTEMPORARY FOREIGN POLICY: ARMAMENTS, COLONIALISM, AND DIPLOMACY

> "Politics is the art of the possible, and the domain of the possible is extremely limited because it is the restricted territory of conflicting interests."—THOMAS MOLNAR

An observer from Mars acquainted with American foreign policy before World War I or in the period between two world wars who returned after 1947 would at first glance probably conclude that the United States had come of age. He would note that after repudiating the international organization which gave reality to President Woodrow Wilson's "Grand Design," Americans recovered by 1946 to help bring into being an international "parliament" now numbering more than eighty member states. Beyond this, he would recall that after the British announced on February 21, 1947, they could no longer fulfil their commitments in Greece and Turkey, President Harry S. Truman on March 12 went before the Congress to ask authority and appropriations not only to fill the vacuum there but "to support free peoples who are resisting attempted subjugation by armed minorities or by outside pressure." Finally, our interplanetary visitor would note that on June 5, 1947, Secretary of

State George C. Marshall in an address at Harvard University announced a major "plan" that in the annals of foreign relations to this day remains synonymous with imagination, inventiveness, and moral courage. This commitment was to involve an American contribution going far beyond our contribution at San Francisco, where at the birth of the United Nations we pledged ourselves to abide by its principles, cast our vote, pay our dues, and perhaps contribute to an international police force if established. Through the Marshall Plan in a little over four years Americans helped Europeans help themselves to restore their economies, recover stable governments, and triumph over the threat of "hunger, poverty, desperation and chaos." Secretary Marshall was careful to say that his policy was "directed not against any country or doctrine" and that aid was available to any European country except those which maneuvered "to block the recovery of other countries." This policy in one of the few such instances following the war placed the Russians on the defensive, left on them the onus of dividing the world if they denied help to the subject peoples under their rule, and found them staging their coup in Czechoslovakia a few days before the Senate was to vote on the program. Mr. Winston S. Churchill described the plan, which provided $17,000,000,000 in aid to Europeans, as the wisest, most unselfish act of any nation in all history.

How are we to think of these steps in recent American policy? In two important respects, one philosophical and the other historical, they are landmarks in America's age-old attempt to come to terms with an external world—a world which intimately affects its life and treasure but which it can never control as it can events within its own boundaries. They are landmarks, I believe, because they represent not perfection but the best men were able to do under the circumstances. Beyond this they stand in a special relationship to at least one philosophy of international relations and to

American history. Philosophically, the pages of history resemble a long and tragic record of man's failure to govern himself and particularly to control his relations with the rest of the world, even though there are moments of greatness for every man and people. You will note throughout that I see the tragic view of life as in many ways closest to reality. It is an outlook that views human history as a succession of Shakespearean dramas with strong men struggling to mitigate or postpone catastrophes which finally no power on earth could resist. Civilizations and societies that attained excellence and approached in some limited way the divine have risen to greatness only to be consumed in defeat and decline. Like it or not, an attitude of irony and pity appears best suited in the long run for a philosophy of nations. History in this perspective is uncomfortably close to Gibbon's harsh but revealing characterization as "little more than the register of the crimes, follies and misfortunes of mankind." Americans as members of a common humanity partaking of all its weaknesses could hardly expect immunity from these shortcomings.

However, the creative measures taken since the close of World War II are notable because they strike a "counterbeat" to the rhythm of a much briefer period in world history. I refer of course to American history with its tiny span of less than two centuries. America's posture in the world has been a product of historical experiences, geographical location, and stubbornly rooted legend and belief. It has persisted because until World War I, it succeeded, in greater or lesser degree, in enabling Americans to conquer the wilderness from the Atlantic seaboard to the Pacific coast, settle and populate a continent, master its natural resources, and emerge as a Great Power. Isolationism as a political doctrine struck deep roots in American soil because it justified a century or more of national conduct and successfully accounted for policies that bore fruit. Indeed, it is obvious that non-participation in world affairs is no American monopoly. It represents one of the classic possibilities open to a people. The neutralist policies of Nehru's India parallel it in our day. Swiss neutrality since 1815 is another expression. So are Britain's "Splendid Isolation" toward continental Europe, especially in the classic period of the balance of power, and Russia's attempt since Peter the Great to be simultaneously part of the European world and a quasi-Asiatic force outside of Europe and opposed to it. Asian examples include China's efforts from 1840 through the first decade of the twentieth century to maintain the symbolic Chinese wall and Japan's isolationism from the early seventeenth to the second half of the nineteenth century.

Doctrines of this kind can of course never be absolute. Men and ideas flowed across the borders of China. The Dutch successfully maintained a trading post at or near Nagasaki throughout Japan's golden era of so-called isolationism. Abstinence from involvement is a limited and fitful stand at best. When Washington in his Farewell Address announced the dictum against entangling alliances, his government had just completed ratification of the Jay Treaty recognizing British rights in commerce, shipping, and maritime matters. Jefferson in his First Inaugural spoke of "peace, commerce and honest friendship with all nations, entangling alliances with none." He added: "Happily for us, the mammoth cannot swim, nor the leviathan move on dry land." Shortly thereafter, as part of one of history's most far-reaching diplomatic undertakings, Jefferson engineered the Louisiana Purchase, negotiated during a period when the clash of the warring governments of France and Great Britain enabled him to achieve his purposes. In 1837 Abraham Lincoln proclaimed in a political address: "All the armies of Europe, Asia, and Africa combined, . . . with a Bonaparte for their commander, could not by force take a drink from the Ohio or make a track on the Blue Ridge in a trial of a hundred years. . . . [Danger] cannot come from abroad." Yet less than a quarter-century before Lincoln spoke, a British army had invaded Washington almost unopposed and had burned down both the Capitol and the White House despite involvement of the major British forces elsewhere in a life-and-death struggle with Napoleon.

Thus isolationism as a doctrine has as often misled as it has illuminated American thinking. Of course this is always the case with legends or doctrines. This country enjoyed for nearly a century and a half an opportunity few nations share to mark out an independent course of action. We were a new nation in a new world beyond the seas. Many of our people had shaken the dust of Europe from their feet and in a new and better homeland they sought release from the anxious and painful strife, the wickedness and frustrations of the old world. They had turned their backs on it forever. In Governor Bradford's words: "The ocean was behind them." A sense of freedom and escape informed their thinking. Europe was the prison-house from which they had fled, America the promised land. Moreover, their sense of escape was reenforced by a pervasive religious and philosophical utopianism. The City of God in the New World had been reached even as the Babylon of the Old World was left behind. The religious ingredient inhered alike in the creed of pilgrims, puritans, and deists. Edward Johnson in *Wonder Working Providence of Zion's Saviour* (1650) spoke of New England as the place "where the Lord would create a new heaven and a new earth, new churches and a new commonwealth together," and Jonathan Edwards, of God's American Israel. Thomas Jefferson in a secularized version of the creed affirmed: "Before the establishment of the American States, nothing was known to history but the man of the old world crowded within limits either small or overcharged and steeped in vices which the situation generates."

It remained for an accompanying philosophical and literary trend of thought to support these beliefs and to take its place among the intellectual forces underlying American thinking. Twenty-four years after Columbus's epoch-making discovery, Sir Thomas More's *Utopia* brought a renaissance of idealized and millennial political thinking. He and the thinkers who followed him discerned in the New World a place where righteousness would dwell. More's was a soul in revolt against the grim realities of the age. "He sees the European states in a condition of veiled and actual hostility; rulers waging wars of aggrandizement; wars breeding other wars and leaving behind a loathesome progeny of hatreds and hardships. . . . Over against the hopeless welter of the Old World he throws up in sharp relief an ideal commonwealth. . . . He pictures Utopia as a larger England, remote and safe from invaders. . . . To lessen the risk of war they make no alliance." [1] Other utopias followed, almost all of them drawing their inspiration from the vision of the "New World" on the west coast of the Atlantic. Bacon's *New Atlantis,* Harrington's *The Commonwealth of Oceana,* Prospero's utopian island in Shakespeare's *The Tempest,* Voltaire's "Eldorado" in *Candide,* and Berkeley's new order where Christian civilization could survive Europe's degeneracy all partake of membership in this tradition. For perhaps the first time, Utopia had a ready-made setting. America *was* Utopia.

Strikingly enough these religious and literary affirmations seemed confirmed by early American history. In the first phase of our history the frontier saved us from the acrimony of class struggle and later our superior technology gave new outlets to the ambitious and adventurous. Beyond this we were freed from international responsibility by the fortuitous coincidence of geographic isolation and a European equilibrium of power which British policy and naval power was

[1] J. Holland Rose and F. R. Salter, "The Old Empire," *The Cambridge History of the British Empire* (Cambridge, 1929), I, 93–95.

dedicated to preserve. In such a world, it was natural to assume that Americans were a chosen people, domestic policies were more important than foreign policies, and alliances so prevalent on the European scene were no more than an expensive and pernicious nuisance. These objective conditions have passed but the psychology lingers on expressed, for example, in sweeping denunciations of the exercise of power by certain European states followed abruptly by the unilateral declaration of readiness to use force, say, in Berlin or the Middle East. The historic American state of mind and sense of mission has been an abiding source of strength in calling men to serve their country. It has also made for that peculiarly American version of self-righteousness about which De Tocqueville wrote:

> If I say to an American that the country he lives in is a fine one, aye, he replies and there is not its equal in the world. If I applaud the freedom its inhabitants enjoy he answers "freedom is a fine thing" but few nations are worthy of it. If I remark on the purity of morals . . . he declares "I can imagine that a stranger who has witnessed the corruption which prevails in other nations would be astonished at the difference." At length I leave him to a contemplation of himself but he returns to the charge and does not desist until he has got me to repeat all I have been saying. It is impossible to conceive a more troublesome and garrulous patriotism.

1. *The Dilemma of Armaments*

This spirit of utopianism and the deeply ingrained tendency to speak in large and absolute terms has continued in American thinking into the mid-twentieth century. Its forms of expression are changing and novel. Isolationism is largely dead, strictures against entangling alliances have been overridden, and nearly two million Americans in fifty-nine countries are engaged in public and private service on a wide front literally encircling the globe. However, the revolution in American foreign policy embodied in the United Nations, the Truman Doctrine, and the Marshall Plan has not been matched by a deepening awareness of international dilemmas. Like children's stories which at an early stage must sharply separate the heroes and the villains for the immature mind, our international approach has its legends of good and bad, "aggressor" and peace-loving states. It is one thing to believe that a people is morally and politically right in a particular course it takes. It is quite another to see this rightness as an inevitable expression of congenital moral superiority or equate rightness or wrongness in the instant case with native virtue and native vice. This view, I might remind you, is hardly confined to international affairs. In the French Revolution some leaders thought that the guillotining of aristocrats would be sufficient to purge France of evil. Marxism in the same spirit calls for the sacrifice of "the exploiters" in the interests of "the people." The American Civil War evoked emotions reminiscent of the French Revolution and the Wars of Religion, and after World War II the destruction and disarming of the evil incarnate in Germany and Japan was viewed as the pathway to peace and justice. We do well to remind one another that another approach is always open to the people and in theory at least was possible after 1945. In such a situation leaders have two choices. To illustrate, in 1814–1815 statesmen might have maintained that France was an aggressor state, that Napoleon's aggressions were nothing more than a repetition of the aggressions of Louis XIV's (as Hitler's were a repetition of the Kaiser's). Instead they chose a second approach. French power was kept intact, and in less than a year of Waterloo France was restored to the counsels of Europe. A remarkable era of a century of peace ensued—at least there was no general war among the five major powers. Is it fair to ask whether the approach of diplomats at the time had anything to do with this nearly unique phenomenon? Was there something lost in spirit and approach between 1815 and 1945?

An alternative to the simple good-and-bad, right-and-wrong approach that all too frequently bedevils American thinking was suggested early in our history by George Washington. He warned that "the nation which indulges toward another an habitual hatred, or an habitual fondness, is, in some degree, a slave." In a similar vein, Nicholas Spykman observed that the charm of international politics is that one never need grow weary of one's friends. In the era of good feeling toward the Russians, Spykman wrote: "A Russian state from the Urals to the North Sea can be no great improvement over a German state from the North Sea to the Urals." In a wartime statement labeled by one critic as something approaching treason, Spykman argued: "The present war effort is undoubtedly directed against the destruction of Hitler and the National Socialist Party, but this does not necessarily imply that it is directed at the destruction of Germany as a military power." [2] This counsel went unheeded and German and Japanese power vacuums were created on either side of the "peace-loving" Soviet Union. As the present Berlin crisis deepens, one cannot stifle the thought that the simple American legend of good and evil men and states has consequences not yet fully measured.

It has fallen to a non-American, the Cambridge historian Herbert Butterfield, to offer a more subtle and satisfying over-all explanation of our international dilemmas. "Behind the great conflicts of mankind," he writes, "is a terrible human predicament. Contemporaries fail to see the predicament or refuse to recognize its genuineness. . . . It is only [later] . . . that men come really to recognize that there was a terrible knot almost beyond the ingenuity of man to

<hr/>

[2] Nicholas J. Spykman, *America's Strategy in World Politics* (New York: Harcourt, Brace and Company, 1942), p. 460.

untie. . . . As regards the real world of international relations I should put forward the thesis . . . that this condition of absolute predicament or irreducible dilemma lies in the very geometry of human conflict." [3] This sense of the human predicament is one that is poignantly expressed in such documents of timeless American statecraft as Lincoln's Second Inaugural Address. It is a sense, however, which is lacking in a more general way when America looks for an over-all philosophy with which to approach its problems. Yet I would suggest it constitutes the only solid and certain ground on which to confront the three massive and fundamental dilemmas to which I propose now to turn.

Historically, since World War II, American foreign policy has cut loose from the moorings of "splendid isolation" and consciously embraced the firm ties of partnership with peoples in Europe and Asia. We have bilateral security arrangements with more than forty nations and our loyalty to the United Nations is beyond dispute. We point to the Marshall Plan as an act of almost unparalleled generosity. Yet the tendency of seeing ourselves as morally and spiritually, if not geographically, apart from the other nations of the world is always present, though hidden beneath the surface, ready to erupt or engulf our thinking. It affects our approach to problems like colonialism, diplomacy, or the use of force, and influences the trend toward a too sanguine point of view about prospects of charting the future. The brutalities, complexities, and uncertainties of foreign relations escape us because of the state of the American mind; and we falter particularly in the realm of means where discriminate judgments, not higher instincts, are at stake.

Not the least of our problems arises precisely with respect to the facts of power, armaments, and force. For more than

[3] Herbert Butterfield has elaborated this theme in a series of writings including *Christianity, Diplomacy and War; History and Human Relations; Christianity and History; Christianity in European History; The Whig Interpretation of History; Man on His Past.*

a century America has proved itself singularly inept in coming to terms with the problems of force. Beginning as early as 1840, there were organized expressions of public feeling proclaiming deep-seated suspicion of diplomacy or force. The "peace movement" had as its goal the substitution of procedures like arbitration or other forms of moral suasion for force. Indeed arbitration was the first of the peace movements to receive governmental sanction. It had served nations well at the turn of the century on issues which had not proved amenable to diplomacy. Settlements like the *Alabama* claims case and Bering Sea fisheries dispute were fresh in the public mind, and it was not surprising that the question should be asked, if settlements like these had been possible, why the same principle should not be applied to all our differences. It was forgotten that states reserve to themselves decisions on matters where vital interests are at stake. The United States itself had refused arbitration on the issue of the sinking of the *Maine,* which touched off the Spanish-American War, and no thoughtful person could have imagined the United States Senate agreeing in advance to bind itself to arbitrate problems involving the Monroe Doctrine or our strategic interests in Panama or the Caribbean.

However, at the turn of the century at both Hague Conferences, the United States delegation pressed for a universal arbitral system. The most important result of the first Hague Conference was the creation of the Permanent Court of Arbitration, which through its selection of panels of judges to serve in individual disputes promised to serve a useful purpose. However, after 1932, in only two cases did the states draw on the resources of the Permanent Court. It came to be supplanted by the Permanent Court of International Justice and the International Court of Justice which were successful primarily in cases of a relatively noninflammable nature. Up to 1959, the present International Court has rendered judgments only in eleven cases. Other arbitration treaties were negotiated; for example, no less than eleven were signed between November 1904 and February 1905. However, in the Senate they were hedged about with restrictions, and Theodore Roosevelt was prompted to say: "Of course it is mere nonsense to have a treaty which does nothing but say that there is no power of enforcing, that whenever we choose, there shall be another arbitration treaty." Because of these objections the agreements were left without senatorial action having been taken. Despite the vigorous efforts of men like Elihu Root, President Taft, and others, they were either not ratified or if ratified remained essentially dead letters. The most elaborate and extensive arrangements were the so-called Bryan Conciliation Treaties negotiated with thirty countries, of which twenty-one were ratified. They provided for conciliation commissions to investigate disputes not susceptible of settlement by diplomatic means and defined a cooling-off period during which the investigation would be carried on. The commissions were envisaged as permanent bilateral bodies to which the respective governments would appoint officials. For the historian the most striking feature of these treaties was that over a period of forty years not a single one was invoked or used in any way. In the period between the wars, an immense body of contractual obligations was evolved in which statesmen assured one another of their resolve not to use force or break the peace. From 1899 to 1933 a total of ninety-seven international agreements for arbitration and conciliation had been negotiated and ratified. It is impossible to appraise the amount of energy and talent that went into this enterprise, but plainly the over-all program was high on the agenda of our international policies. Yet aside from certain private disputes that scarcely had international significance, only two outstanding international problems were arbitrated, and ironically no general arbitration treaty was necessary in either of these cases. One was the North Atlantic Fisheries dispute between the United States and Great Britain involving interpretation of the provisions of a ninety-year-old treaty. The other concerned the question of sovereignty over the island of Palmas and arose from a dispute between the United States and the Netherlands. These two cases are the entire return on the prodigious efforts of American leaders and in particular Secretaries of State Bryan, Kellogg, and Stimson. It should also be noted that events which threatened to shatter the fabric of international society were taking place simultaneously with the efforts at legislating arbitration. At the time of the first Hague Conference, Russia was extending its influence into Manchuria; the final stage of the battle of the Marne coincided with the signing of four conciliation treaties in Washington; and the attempts by Kellogg and Stimson took place as Hitler's star was rising in Germany, the First Five-Year Plan was unfolding in Russia, and the Japanese were pushing into Manchuria. It would be difficult to show that these events were affected even in the slightest by such an approach to the problem of force. More dramatic than this were the efforts at disarmament and, climactically, at the outlawry of war, but the fanfare and moral enthusiasm surrounding them were in no sense commensurate with their usefulness as restraints on power.

In the aftermath of World War II, force once again has confounded policy-makers. The early postwar treaties were conceived of as means by which wartime partnership could be extended into the peace. Yet the disparity between Western power and the force in being of the Soviet Union, especially its distribution in Europe, played havoc with attempts at erecting a viable peace. The only crime of Yalta was the failure to recognize soon enough the intimate connection between power and peace—a failure for which we all are at least partly responsible. If this failing were not deeply embedded in our contemporary national character, we might have been less willing to see the basis destroyed for a viable settlement of the Suez crisis where we have since 1956 carried on negotiations with Colonel Nasser more from weakness than strength.

The problems of power have obviously been magnified by the sharp rise in the magnitude of force. Nearly four decades ago the Right Honorable Herbert Asquith observed that science was beginning to "lisp the alphabet of annihilation." The dangers are daily borne in upon us not only of mutual devastation in war but also of radioactive poison in peace. In the hydrogen era our approach to the problem of force has been curiously reminiscent of earlier days. The number of words and proposals devoted to a generalized attack on the disarmament problem perhaps exceeds attention to any comparable problem. Whereas before World War II the approach was one of erecting a system of fixed legal and arbitral procedures culminating in broad over-all legislation outlawing war—the Kellogg-Briand Pact—the postwar design has called for almost endless exchanges with Soviet delegates within the United Nations and outside, all looking toward the banning of the use of force at least in certain of its forms.

The dread disease which has tended to paralyze American thinking on the problem of force has its roots in at least three conditions of the American mind. We have assumed that force could be dealt with in the isolated compartments of disarmament conventions or arbitral treaties divorced from the harsh realities of power in the outside world or from viable strategic doctrines evolved to meet mutual interests and needs. We have favored a legal over a diplomatic approach. We have preferred to think in absolute rather than discriminate terms and to see force as a single-edged weapon that might be drawn in a violent cause. In consequence, perhaps there is no area of international life where success has been more fleeting and where the best efforts of men supremely endowed have been greeted with more modest achievements. Only the strong currents of the American approach to world problems and our yearning for over-all formulas have kept afloat this mode of dealing with force.

The first of our dilemmas arises because of the central place that armaments and power continue to hold in world politics today. This is true despite the revolution in weapons with which we are confronted.

The military establishments of nations remain possibly the most explicit element of foreign policy. Diplomacy and military strength appear to go hand in hand. In an earlier day the great powers sent gunboats up the rivers of states they were seeking to influence. Today in the cold war the postwar distribution of power is closely related to the position of the Red Army at strategic points in the heart of Europe. Germany's demonically successful diplomacy in the interwar period must be seen as the direct outgrowth of superior military preparedness. The explosion and testing of atomic weapons by the Soviet Union has been joined with periodic and deliberately calculated strategic moves in the cold war, and our own technological advances have similarly been used to exert influence on the Russians. Oftentimes the frontiers separating the spheres of influence of warring states demarcate the limits of their effective military force— for example, in Korea. As long as force remains the final arbiter of rivalries among nations, the comparative strengths of their military establishments set boundaries to their actions in foreign affairs.

Military strength quite obviously lacks the fixed quality or relative permanence of other elements of foreign policy like geography or natural resources. It has been subject throughout history to the compulsions of technological change, and military history is replete with examples of military techniques that have supplanted one another and brought far-reaching shifts in power. The phalanx was the key to Sparta's victory over Athens in the Peloponnesian War of 431–404 B.C. Its effectiveness lay in the use of heavy infantry in close-order formation and reliance upon shock techniques. The Athenians recovered from their defeat and thirty-three years later employed swarms of light infantry to conquer the Spartans. Somewhat later the Thebans improved the phalanx by distributing its power in depth, thus introducing an element of surprise which had been missing. The Macedonians revamped the Spartan phalanx, made use of Greek mercenaries, and put their stress on a war of movement. But Macedonia was succeeded by the military genius and mobile legions of Rome. Hardened in civil and border wars, the Roman army proved versatile enough to fight as skirmishers or heavy armed infantrymen in open country and in villages and towns. However, the battle of Adrianople against heavy armed cavalrymen from the east brought the challenge Roman military leaders had foreseen but for which they were unprepared. In modern times technology has given dramatic opportunities to military leaders who proved capable of adaptation and innovation. By contrast, failure to respond to change has usually meant failure even for those whose traditional military resources appeared to be adequate. Thus the Germans, using the strategy of 1870, were defeated in World War I by their opponent's order of battle of trench warfare and economic blockade. The French in the 1930's, expecting another costly and brutal war of attrition, built the Maginot Line to fight the kind of struggle which military technology had already rendered obsolete. Short of warfare itself, the failure of military establishments to keep pace with fast moving technological changes can also reduce the influence of nations in the chancelleries of the world. This in effect was the tragedy of France before World War II.

The difficulties inherent in maintaining military establishments that will not suffer defeat are more complex than mere response to technological change. A nation may clearly recognize the need for military organs capable of supporting the foreign policies it pursues but be limited in the margin of its economic resources that can be turned to military use. Some countries exhaust their resources in attaining a viable economy; others like the United States have a surplus with which to meet foreign military and political commitments. Belgium cannot afford to devote the same part of its gross national product to military ends as can the Soviet Union or the United States. Thus, both in absolute and relative terms, the military establishment of smaller powers, including the newer states, must lag behind.

If the present crisis between East and West were a simple clash either of military systems or of political ideologies, we should doubtless face the future with greater confidence and hope. However, honest men admit that most of us vacillate between a military and ideological view of the struggle. The problem of arriving at valid and acceptable policies is at root the problem of defining the nature of the crisis. The uncertainty we feel about policies is basically an uncertainty over the crisis. There is irony in this perplexity because most informed observers in the early days of the cold war were convinced that the Russian threat to Western civilization— although its tactics differed—was identical in its effects on the world balance of power with the Nazi menace. As such, the recipe for dealing with it was assumed to be the same. It was said that if our leaders had occasion to learn anything from over two centuries of national experience, it was that foreign policy divorced from strength is likely to be impotent. Following two world wars, the United States dismantled its military establishment as an earnest of its peaceful intentions and good will. In both cases, aggressive forces bent on expansion seized on such acts to press forward into areas defenseless against their power. Both Germany and the Soviet Union imposed their will upon helpless nations that fell within their zone of control.

The lesson this taught Western leaders was that weakness could be no substitute for security, that policies harnessed to power were more likely to succeed than those drawing strength from high ideals and noble expectations alone. Belgium in World War I and the Baltic States in World War II succumbed, not because they were lacking in morality, but because they found no means of securing their national frontiers.

The West has carried this discovery into the atomic and thermonuclear age. It is possible to argue that such peace as we have known since 1945 is the outcome of a "balance of terror." There are signs that the Soviet Union more than once marched up to the brink, threatening to engulf Greece and Turkey, Iran and Berlin, only to march down again when it met resistance. Conversely, where resistance proved ambiguous, uncertain, or divided, as in Egypt, Syria, and in the Far East, the spread of the Soviet sphere of influence flowed across boundaries that had long marked the limits of Russian power.

Seen from this approach, the immediate military threat is unquestionably the gravest danger. Those who hold to this view call for ever greater urgency in the multiplication of more powerful weapons of destruction, for new strategic doctrines, and for missile bases and a nuclear weapons pool. The irreconcilable conflicts and tensions of the "cold war" will come to an end only when one side or the other forges decisively ahead. Power finally will arbitrate the rivalry and the foe in the end will surrender unconditionally. This trend of thought prompts a state to bestow the most lethal weapons on its allies. When the allies show reluctance at being caught in the crossfire of two atomic powers, the state bargains over commitments "in principle" and makes concessions in order that the morality of power will prevail.

At war with this first approach is a second that urges us to display equal vision and energy in seeking political and economic solutions as in launching expanded military programs. It points to the Soviet technical assistance program pledging $1.5 billion to the underdeveloped areas and to the evidence of successful Soviet penetration into the Middle East. The scene and tactics of Russian imperialism have shifted. Subversion, infiltration, and indirect aggression (disguised as appeals to anticolonialism, anti-interventionism, and anti-Westernism) have put the West on the defensive perhaps on its weakest front.

Ultimate weapons in these areas are bound to have ambiguous effects, since their use against great numbers of agrarian peoples spread over vast areas seems doubtful at best. Crises that have passed without their employment in Indo-China, Korea, and Egypt serve to reinforce such doubts. Because they neither possessed nor saw the relevance of these terrible weapons, the newer nations have led the movement for their outlawry.

However, the contradictory reactions in the newer states to thermonuclear devices is best seen in the effects of the sputniks. In the same countries that urge us to disarm, American prestige and virtue suffered a grievous blow when the Soviet Union launched the first satellite. Despite continuous criticism of America throughout Asia and Africa for its materialism and preoccupation with purely technological and military advance, confidence in American policy was gauged by these very standards so deplored. One is reminded once more of Europe's and Asia's response when the United States, through the United Nations, held the line in Korea. Then our sharpest critics (including some in India who had found us rigidly anti-Communist and obsessed with the military threat) applauded the successful employment of American power, particularly until the fateful crossing of the 38th parallel.

The issue between the two approaches is not one that can be measured and appraised by a barometer of the rise and fall of Stalinism in the Soviet Union. If Stalinism means a brutal and heedless sacrifice of every goal to the goals of the Communist society, Stalinism lives as much today as ever. However, the fact is that Stalin no less than his successors pursued Russian objectives along more than one front— even though the accent on economic-political warfare seems recently to have increased. It is undeniably the case that the Russian military threat survives the death of Stalin; and if anyone has any doubt, he need only look to the sputniks, to the stress on force, and to the hundreds of Russian divisions guarding Soviet frontiers. Or he can listen to the threats and counterthreats of the Russian tyrants brandishing the instruments of force at each emerging crisis, e.g., the Suez crisis, Hungary, Poland, and the Turkish-Syrian and the Berlin disputes. But the countless moves and countermoves on the political and economic front are equally real; and with Soviet tactics of advance and retreat, the contest shifts almost imperceptibly from one type of warfare to another or sometimes is joined simultaneously on all sides. The greatest risk an observer can run is to exclude one or the other dimension of the crisis in his zeal to describe reality in shades of black and white.

Assuming then that the present crisis is partly but not exclusively military in nature, there are other problems to be faced. Three errors are commonly made in appraising the military component of foreign policy. First, military power is often confused with national power, and a nation's capacity to impose its will is equated with its military establishment. By contrast, military power is like the fist whose force depends on the health and vitality of the body politic and the whole society. Troops in being are an important determinant of a successful foreign policy, but without other foundations they will not suffice. Second, the military element is often viewed in more static terms than is appropriate. The democracies in two world wars, while they have been the last to arm, have rallied their forces to gain victory in the end. Third, it is difficult to analyze and foresee the most effective distribution of the components of military force. For example, what comprises a strong military force today? Is it large ground forces, hydrogen bombs, or intensive research? Is a small, highly specialized army more desirable than large ground forces, or are both essential for a nation that seeks to be strong? The answers to these questions will probably be decisive in determining future influence in the world of states, yet it is sobering that estimates must be made on the basis of contingencies that cannot be foreseen. We know in a general way that an effective foreign policy must be supported by a military program that can safeguard national security. But this leaves those who make decisions with the painful task of distributing resources among alternative means of defense without any certainty of the kind of war they may have to fight.

Beyond this, the weapons of today may not be used in future wars because technology has rendered them obsolete. It is said that conventional weapons are fast being supplanted by new and more deadly weapons and therefore traditional armaments fail to provide an adequate basis for foreign policy. On the other hand, there are military experts who question whether atomic and hydrogen weapons will ever be used, given the prospect of mutual annihilation. Is it not fair then to ask whether the stockpiling of an unlimited supply of weapons that no nation would dare to use furnishes a state with the requisite military support? If so, a military establishment grounded in conventional weapons may fall short of providing a defensible military posture, but so may a policy aimed at superior atomic capacities. These are the horns of the dilemma on which, for the moment at least, defense strategists find themselves impaled.

2. *The Dilemma of Colonialism*

Another set of problems stems from the colonial dilemma which reaches beyond our national life and touches conflicting interests at work in the world at large. It has been obvious since World War II that the colonial problem stands at the top of almost every agenda for discussion of American foreign policy. New nations in the throes of birth-pangs are appearing in Asia, Africa, and the Middle East. The effect of widespread popular attention here and abroad has been to draw from responsible officials impassioned proclamations on Western policy. We are asked by some to define our policy on the colonial problem and to throw our weight behind popular revolutions. Others charge we are both "a pillar of society and a patron of revolution."

In this setting it is tempting and sometimes perhaps essential that we take general and sweeping positions and answer the call to express an American doctrine on the rights of peoples everywhere to independence and self-government. This is particularly true because our own experience is so rich in lessons and apparently pregnant with meaning. The fruits of attempts thus far to propound a dogma should serve, however, to give us pause, for the record of America's efforts to align itself squarely with either colonial or anticolonial powers is sprinkled both with failures and successes.

Nevertheless, we face new situations today and demands crowd in upon us for new and more vigorous policies. We are reminded that Senator Vandenburg, with his emphasis on Europe and Western unity, never disparaged the rights of colonial or former colonial peoples. Nationalism is on the march in the far-flung reaches of the world, and the more enlightened American citizens implore one another to identify America with these movements rather than continually appearing to stand in their pathway. Unhappily, the colonial problem is more intractable than those exhortations suggest. For at the same time we seek to end old imperialisms, a new and more demoniac expansionism threatens us. To meet it we must cleave to our trusted friends and allies with whom we have interests and military bases in common and strive to preserve a more stable world balance of power. Yet, in itself, this position is not enough. The present equilibrium of power will eventually be upset unless we can join with new forces in the so-called underdeveloped areas. We may say, therefore, that the United States faces the triple challenge of stemming the tide of Russian imperialism and world communism, uniting the other Western states, and drawing closer to non-Western peoples only recently emerging as independent states. In a manner of speaking, policymakers must keep three balls in the air. This is the unenviable task of American statesmanship.

The pathos of our present position may be illustrated briefly from a few recent events in American history. First there was the statement on Goa by Mr. Dulles supporting Portugal's rights in the tiny enclave on the sprawling subcontinent of India. It was prompted doubtless by the zeal of European officers in the State Department to display a sense of community with Portugal. Everyone knows it provoked deep resentment in India and perhaps throughout much of Asia. Next came the public expression of "sympathy" for Greek feelings in the Cyprus dispute by our Ambassador to Greece, Cavendish W. Cannon, which unleashed a torrent of British protest. Shortly thereafter the Dutch voiced dismay at Mr. Dulles' warm and friendly comments during a visit to the Indonesian Republic. More recently, we aroused our European friends by appearing to take sides with Egypt. Taken together, our several efforts to cement ties of community and good will with one side in the colonial struggle by bold official affirmations threatened or ruptured the bonds of unity with the other. Possibly the one exception was the speech of Douglas Dillon, then Ambassador in Paris, supporting France's search for "liberal solutions" of her problems in North Africa, and even it was challenged by the moderate Tunisian nationalist leader Bourguiba.

Perceiving these problems, is there anything one can say about this perplexing picture which will offer some guidance to the juggler or policy-maker of whom I have spoken? Are there guidelines or principles we can enunciate to spotlight a few of the murkier and more obscure corners of this colonial problem? I believe there are. First, we must start with the presumption that the colonial problem is fraught with dilemmas with which we must learn to live. Nor will dogmas for or against colonialism waft them away. Solutions must be worked out case by case; and as, for example, Tunisia is not identical with Algeria, policies must be shaped to meet individual needs. Secondly, timing is of the essence. The statement supporting Indonesia stirred up a hornet's nest because of Dutch-Indonesian tensions at this time arising partly from the trial of a former Chief of Dutch Military Intelligence charged with plotting to overthrow the Indonesian government, partly from the conflict over Netherlands New Guinea, and partly from the unilateral abridgment by Indonesia of certain financial and economic treaties. If we propose to affirm American support of a disputing state, the style and timing of our statements is as important as the substance. Thirdly, if any general solution can be found, it rests as a rule in the co-ordinating of mutual interests, not in the wholesale sacrifice of one set of interests to another. In North Africa, French, American, and African interests appear to coincide as respects "liberal solutions." Likewise in other regions the goal should be the harmonizing of interests. This calls for a judicious balancing of claims, not for placing one set above all others. Fourthly, it is one of the ironies of history that force may sometimes be necessary to preserve colonial arrangements not in order to perpetuate them but that their orderly liquidation may be achieved. Yet in the end, especially when force is the sole response, it must fail in its purpose. Fifth, it will not do to call every conflict of views between ourselves and our European allies a colonial issue. On October 2, 1956, in what one commentator called a Freudian slip that betrayed the main lines of American thinking, Mr. Dulles noted that Britain and America were at odds over Suez on the question of the "shift from colonialism to independence." He treated Suez as an issue between the "colonial powers" and "the powers which are primarily and uniquely concerned with the problem of getting their independence as rapidly as possible." Walter Lippmann was prompt to point out that Egypt could hardly be considered a colony, particularly as it sought to expand the sphere of its national power. A British journal observed: "The American desire to keep the goodwill of the Arab states is good sense . . . but it will defeat itself in the end if, in pursuing it, the Americans think in anti-colonial conventions which are current. . . . In that way they will merely seek to please everybody, committing their strength to the support of local weak men, and overlooking that the conflicts which trouble the region, being real conflicts, require solutions of substance which are bound to give offense to some." Finally, conflicts of interest—as in the past between Britain and India or the Dutch and the Indonesians—may be swept along by powerful historical movements until one side emerges supreme. Here it may be necessary for American policy-makers to choose sides and in this way finally and inevitably give offense. These facts need not preclude restraint, but they do set certain guidelines within which policy must be worked out. The guidelines themselves are malleable as one set of forces and claims may overwhelm others and force lines of action we may not have sensed were necessary before.

In principle the United States has been firmly and solidly anticolonial whenever national interest allowed. Our creed is stated unequivocally in the founding document which begins: "When in the course of human events it becomes necessary for one people to dissolve the political bands which have connected them with another. . . ." It was easier to announce this doctrine when the prime American objective was to keep the European colonial powers from the shores of the Western Hemisphere. When American power and responsibilities expanded to other continents and the need increased for collaboration with friends and allies in Europe, freedom to affirm our purposes was more sharply circumscribed. President Franklin D. Roosevelt, despite his unquenchable devotion to freedom and national self-determination, felt this most acutely. The Atlantic Charter was a means of his affirming "the rights of all peoples to choose the form of government under which they will live." He vowed he would see that the signatories met this pledge as he had earlier proclaimed: "There has never been, there isn't now, and there never will be any race of people on earth fit to serve as masters over their fellow men. . . . We believe that any nationality, no matter how small, has the inherent right to its own nationhood." [4] Yet Roosevelt's ambitious and noble design for a colonial "new deal" ran athwart of the claims of the Joint Chiefs of Staff for island bases among the former Japanese mandated territories. Additionally, he saw, as did his Secretary of State Cordell Hull, the impossibility of alienating European allies when co-operation in peace and war was the cornerstone of American policy. It had been comparatively simple to declare anticolonialism to the world when the United States carried limited burdens. The Grand Alliance if it were to stand the test of time required an

[4] Franklin D. Roosevelt, "Address to the White House Correspondents Association in 1941," quoted by F. R. Dulles and G. E. Riginger, "Anti-Colonial Policies of FDR," *Political Science Quarterly*, LXX (March 1955), 1–18.

accommodation of our principles to the interests we shared with the British and some of the European states.

Since 1945 the United States perforce has been more often mediator than champion in the colonial struggle. Sometimes, when possessing freedom of action, the United States could grant statehood to the Philippines, but more often as in Indochina and Indonesia our task was to help the parties to inch toward a more viable solution. When we tipped the scale toward one side or another, we did so with restraint and caution and reassured the contending forces: "We are not sitting in judgment on a case in which one or the other party has brought about a failure. . . ." Some might accuse us of fence-straddling but the truth of the matter was that our principles were being applied in circumstances that denied full freedom to choose one set of national purposes to the exclusion of others. We found on occasion we had underestimated the strength of two sets of claims, each carrying some elements of legitimacy within the assumptions on which they were based. If "politics is a process of the slow boring of hard wood," the American policies pursued were probably inevitable. The protagonists in almost every struggle were four in number. The colonial powers maintained that economic survival required raw materials to meet chronic economic shortages and essential bases for defense which they could point out were essential both for themselves and for the defense of Western civilization. The Afro-Asian bloc asserted that peace and any vestiges of colonialism were utterly incompatible. The communists sought to exploit every ambition and fear and the United States, wedded simultaneously to anti-colonialism and to Europe, was caught in a dreadful position of contradiction and paradox that even clever verbal alchemy could not obscure or erase.

No one has discovered any means of escape from the colonial dilemma. It remains a problem with which public and policy-makers must learn to live. We may find certain guidelines, but more profoundly, the beginning of wisdom is the knowledge that this is a persisting dilemma we face at least for any foreseeable future.

3. The Dilemma of Democratic Diplomacy

In turning from the two problems I have been discussing to the third, I should perhaps lay bare a personal conviction. I believe that Americans, including isolationists, have in the main awakened to the central relationship between force and foreign policy, although ironically enough at a moment when it takes on the greatest ambiguity and complexity. I remind you, for example, that Congressmen are speaking out more unqualifiedly than responsible officials in the executive branch. They have urged mounting expenditures for building up a whole panoply of the instruments of defense, and this in spite of their accountability to political constituencies for rising taxes. War colleges and institutes for research on national defense launch a steady stream of new insights and imaginative formulations, and the number of books and conferences proliferates from year to year. Similarly, colonialism and the choices open to American policymakers in one form or another constitute a focus for inquiry and discussion at many points around the country. It is the third dilemma that has been largely neglected by Americans except for a handful of former practitioners and scholarly analysts. I refer of course to the dilemma of diplomacy in the modern world.

It is essentially a dilemma created by the changing conditions and realities of modern life. On one hand, diplomacy has for the first time in history become the business of all the people. You will remember that until 1914 the conduct of international relations was the task of the professionals, and few people gave it heed. This state of affairs ended abruptly with World War I when particularly in this country a powerful campaign was launched to popularize international politics and thereby rid the world of strife. War was widely attributed to the wickedness of governments and, more specifically, to the nefarious role of secret treaties. A philosophy of international relations was born and flourished which because of its simplicity and directness engendered widespread popular appeal—an appeal that continues to the present day. It was a philosophy which in a spirit of buoyant optimism looked to democracy and national self-determination as twin sources of international peace and order. The creation of popular regimes on the Anglo-American model throughout the world was heralded as the sure corrective to those harsh conflicts that for centuries had wracked international life. Once the numerous subject peoples had achieved political societies reflecting the popular will, their ancient rivalries with "oppressor" states and the struggles between conflicting dominions warring over territorial claims would come to an end. The unquenchable faith of contemporary Western *homo sapiens* in man's potentialities for progress spiraling ever upward found expression in assurances that a brave new world merely awaited the fulfilment of these goals.

However, faith in the future has had its roots not only in democracy and national self-determination; it also resides in the confidence that novel international institutions have rendered diplomacy obsolete. Implicit here is a belief that the certainty of progress is waiting at the other end of a charter, a constitution, or a court judgment. The United Nations emerges in the minds of some of its American champions as an organization that may confidently be expected to do away with alliances, balance of power, secret diplomacy, and state rivalries. In the *Report of the Advisory Committee on International Relations* of the Social Science Research Council, Professor James Shotwell could write of "new forms arising which . . . will modify the entire relationship of civilized nations." In *Essays on the Social Gospel,* Adolf Harnack declared: "Retrogression is no longer possible for us; and shame on those who desire it." [5] This sanguine and unquestioning outlook which envisaged the transformation of international behavior through multilateralism reinforced and strengthened the faith in democracy and self-determination. It almost inevitably gave to the study of diplomacy—its forms, principles and problems—the flavor of an inferior and even slightly unpatriotic intellectual activity. It made the traditional diplomat a sinister and suspicious figure caught up in duplicity and double-dealing.

History has dealt harshly with these two viewpoints and, in the recent past, faith in them has been rudely shaken. The phenomenon of totalitarian democracy, unknown in the nineteenth century, has not only left political rivalries and conflict intact but has heightened and made virtually irreconcilable disputes among new collectivities. Inflamed public passions playing on statesmen have made moderation and compromise more difficult of attainment. National leaders in turn by pandering to popular passions have narrowed the alternative courses of action open to them. Nationalism, far from bringing the millennium, has bred bitter antagonisms between new nations and former colonial masters or between non-Western states and their erstwhile exemplars in the West. It has also become a weapon both sides have employed in the struggles of the Cold War.

National self-determination, multilateralism, and democracy can hardly be said to have ushered in a new era. Indeed our more serious observers find deep anguish in the steep and sudden decline of influence and self-confidence among Western democracies. Whatever its goals or purposes, the West succeeds in engendering resentment and suspicion more often than it earns respect. Yet many students and statesmen in-

---

[5] Adolf Harnack and Wilhelm Hermann, *Essays on the Social Gospel* (New York: G. P. Putnam's Sons, 1906), p. 7.

sist on talking in bated breath about the causes and conditions of our decline. The bulk of those who assume leadership in intellectual and political life are singularly inhibited when it comes to diagnosing the sources of our ills. It is commonplace to respond to questions touching the conduct of democratic foreign policy by pointing the finger at nondemocratic societies still more obviously the authors of recent historic catastrophes.

The key to these difficult problems is clearly not loss of faith in democracy. Nor is it the denial of progress as such. It is progress as perfectibility that is questioned. History is the record of significant human advances, but advances marred by retreat and retrogression as well. Furthermore, progress more often than not is the half-step, the partial advance that is accepted even though the ultimate goal falls just beyond reach. This truth is one that wise men perceive, and in perceiving make their contribution to progress.

The truth with which we must learn to live is that democratic and multilateral diplomacy, like all diplomacy, must adhere to certain sound principles and rules, many of which have stood the test of time. At critical key points there must be consistency with the imperatives of the diplomatic tradition. Majority votes in multilateral conferences, and dialectics, invective, or propaganda may hold a certain fascination for spectators of world affairs. More often than not, however, their effect is to sow international distrust and increase rather than alleviate world tensions. Experiences in the United Nations of a little more than a decade have left us a deposit of basic if sometimes neglected object lessons.

For the better part of four centuries the statecraft of Europe displayed certain salient features. In theory at least, it sought to mitigate and reduce conflicts by means of persuasion, compromise, and adjustment. It was a diplomacy rooted in the community of interests of a small group of leaders who spoke the same language, catered as often to one another as to their own people, and played to one another's strengths and weaknesses. When warfare broke out, they drew a ring around the combatants and sought to localize and neutralize the struggle. The old diplomacy, so-called, carried on its tasks in a world made up of states that were small, separated, limited in power, and blessed, ironically enough, by half-hearted political loyalties. Patience was a watchword; negotiations were as protracted during war as in peace. Everyone took for granted that negotiations and talks would be initiated, broken off, resumed, discontinued temporarily, and reopened again by professionals in whose lexicon there was no substitute for "diplomacy."

Today not one of these conditions is any longer present and the quest for new techniques and formulas in the conduct of diplomacy has gone on apace. In part these new formulas stem from the magnitude of international business. For several decades following the Civil War, the tasks of the American Secretary of State were carried on with sufficient leisure so he could combine them with part-time legal practice. One recalls the comment of an earlier Secretary of State, Thomas Jefferson, that for over two years nothing had been heard from the Ambassador to Madrid. If another year brought no word, Jefferson proposed to contact him. The state machinery for international affairs has also been greatly expanded. The American Foreign Service as late as 1929 numbered 3,000 officials while today more than 20,000 are on its rosters. Every day a dozen or more international conferences are in session with an American delegation present fortified by staff and instructions. It is no exaggeration to say that every few minutes of every day some American delegate is asked to express American policy at an international meeting at some point on the globe. Secretary Dulles during the first ten months of office met with a committee or subcommittee of Congress on no less than seventy occasions. Instantaneous systems of communication and rapid means of transportation literally make the modern diplomat a "minute man." One recalls that Secretary of State Dulles received word of the 1958 revolution in Iraq in the early morning hours of July 14, and almost immediately the world awaited a response from the leading free world power. Reactions that in earlier decades could be deliberate, measured, and gradually worked out must now be formulated with the same dispatch as the orders of a company commander in World War II. Consider the speed with which President Eisenhower and Premier Khrushchev have fired salvos in their continuing war of words.

The first and most novel pattern of diplomacy to crystallize since 1945 found expression in the United Nations and in affiliated agencies of "public diplomacy." For the tortuous paths of traditional diplomacy it substituted international forums. Public diplomacy reflects an all-pervasive faith in parliamentary procedures, in the rule of the people, and in straightforward, rational exchange among all nations. It translates into global terms the supreme political attainments of free people within the democratic state. It stands as the very antithesis of secret diplomacy by a concert of leaders of the pre-eminent countries.

The resemblance to national parliaments of even the strongest and most universal world institution, the United Nations, can be misleading. For example, the General Assembly can listen and recommend but it cannot legislate. Its Councils and Secretariat and the International Court of Justice are executive and judicial organs only in the most limited and restricted sense. Secretary Dag Hammarskjold has reasoned: "A voting victory in a national legislature leads to decisions which have the force of law. The legislative process in the United Nations, on the other hand, leads only to the passage of recommendations which do not have the force of law." [6] Because of this fact "The legislative process in the United Nations is not a substitute for diplomacy. It serves its purpose only when it helps diplomacy to arrive at agreements between the national states concerned." [7] The Secretary General concludes: "Since the legislative processes of the United Nations do not lead to legislation . . . the value of public debate in the U.N. can be measured only by the degree to which it contributes to the winning of agreement by the processes of diplomacy. If public debate contributes to winning consent either immediately or in the long run, it serves the purpose of peace-making. If it does not so contribute, then it may be a useless, or even harmful exercise." [8]

A preliminary and highly tentative estimate of popular diplomacy may perhaps be in order considering it has been the keyboard on which so much of postwar diplomacy has been played. The problems of "diplomacy in a goldfish bowl" or, in Ernest Bevin's phrase, diplomacy in "the bear pit," frequently take on a stubbornly intractable quality that many United Nations architects could scarcely have anticipated. Publicity has been both a virtue and a vice. It has kept the spotlight of public opinion on world affairs, but it has also encouraged actors, in striking a pose for national publics, to take inflexible positions from which retreat or compromise proved impossible. Majority votes on South Africa, Hungary, and Korea demonstrated who controlled the greatest support. However, these votes have often allowed conflicts of interest to persist or have actually contributed to the increase of tensions. When this new pattern of diplomacy has worked, it generally has been combined with more ancient techniques, as in the private diplomacy of Ralph

[6] Secretary General Dag Hammarskjold, "The Element of Privacy in Peace-Making," Address at Ohio University, Athens, Ohio, Feb. 5, 1958, Press Release SG/656, United Nations Department of Public Information, p. 3.
[7] Ibid.
[8] Ibid., p. 5.

Bunche in Palestine, Philip C. Jessup on Berlin, and, most notably, the "quiet diplomacy" of the present Secretary General.

Mr. Hammarskjold is at least as conscious of these problems as any of his contemporaries. In the Introduction to the Secretary-General's Tenth Annual Report, he writes: "Within the framework of the charter there are many possibilities, as yet largely unexplored, for variation of practice. The United Nations is at a very early stage in that development of constitutional life based on the written word which is familiar and normal in the life of nations. It is my hope that solid progress can be made in the coming years in developing new forms of contact, new methods of deliberation, and new techniques of reconciliation." One senses a growing feeling that public debate is a drastic process and ought not be used for casual and frivolous purposes. Debate and demands for a vote are a substitute for more violent steps like war, not for less dangerous techniques like negotiations. Sir Leslie Munro reports that the major accomplishment of his term in the autumn of 1957 as President of the General Assembly was the Turkish-Syrian dispute in which the temptation to pass a resolution or call for a vote was resisted. Instead the discussions served as a kind of a poultice for extracting inflammation and reducing the fever of the conflict. In this sense, discussion and debate however prolonged, discouraging, and apparently pointless may sometimes be a useful and, I am told, even a deliberate device for gaining the time in which tensions may subside. United Nations processes may have played a similar role in the conflict between India and Pakistan over Kashmir—a conflict that threatened at several points to flare into open violence. Dean Rusk, whose writings carry their wisdom lightly, observes: "There is utility in tedium, and I suspect that we could use more of it in the conduct of our foreign policy. . . . Success in the conduct of our foreign affairs is to be measured not in tally sheets, but by issues satisfactorily resolved, friendships consolidated, rivalries reduced or circumscribed." [9]

The tempering and limiting of the worst excesses of public diplomacy has not forestalled a countertendency. This tendency is of course foreshadowed in President Franklin D. Roosevelt's personal diplomacy before and during World War II. The Eisenhower administration has espoused "personal diplomacy" as a corrective to "diplomacy in the goldfish bowl." The first Geneva Conference, the United States–Canadian–Mexican Conference at White Sulphur Springs, and the meeting with India's Prime Minister Nehru and Britain's Prime Minister Macmillan illustrate a new and emerging pattern. It is a pattern ostensibly based upon the President's partiality "for talking things out rather than negotiating things out." It reflects the view that many of the abrasive causes of friction can be blunted and dissolved when leaders from other nations, sitting across a table from Mr. Eisenhower, become persuaded of his good intentions. The personal touch of a famous personality at his best in an atmosphere of genial informality is placed on the scales of world diplomacy.

Personal diplomacy is further a present-day household word because of the proclivities of recent American Secretaries of State, particularly Mr. John Foster Dulles. In one respect, diplomacy has come full circle since the days when prince addressed himself to prince without benefit of diplomatic intermediaries. Both the President and Secretary pride themselves on direct contacts with foreign leaders. In Mr. Dulles' words: "I fly because I go to meet heads of government, foreign ministers of other countries, and in a few minutes or at most few hours of personal consultation you can achieve a much better understanding than you can possibly achieve by going through the processes of communicat-

[9] Dean Rusk, "Parliamentary Diplomacy—Debate vs. Negotiation," *World Affairs Interpreter*, XXVI, No. 2 (Summer 1955), 137.

ing through notes and writing to each other." [10] The belief is current that when two reasonable men sit down together, the difficulties that have loomed large in correspondence may suddenly evaporate.

In two important respects, personal diplomacy has changed the character of the diplomatic art. On one hand, the role of the professional diplomat or ambassador tends to be downgraded. In a crisis, the State Department may rush in the Secretary or a high ranking trouble-shooter. The Ambassador runs the risk of becoming a glorified handy man or messenger boy either whispering into the ear of his minister flying in and departing by jet stream or carrying the latest set of documents between the State Department and another country's foreign office. On the other hand, the independence and authority, judgment and maneuver historically open to professional diplomats have been sharply cut back. Lester B. Pearson, sensing this, has asked: "Where do all these developments leave the professional? . . . Are they now mere ciphers to give cocktail parties, to meet planes and to entertain Congressmen . . . ?" He notes: "Before the twentieth century, Ministers devoted their time and energy to working out policy on the advice of their experts. . . . Ambassadors executed these policies . . . and by their manner of doing so . . . often influenced them." [11] Now the process has been drastically altered. For example, in the past, the groundwork was laid for every important settlement through patient and protracted efforts carried on through established diplomatic channels. The preliminary soundings and orderly exchanges by duly authorized representatives in embassies abroad frequently carried negotiations to the point where all that remained for executives and ministers was the ratification of agreements carefully prepared at the working diplo-

---

[10] Quoted by Dana Adams Schmidt, "Instant Diplomacy and the New Diplomats," *Columbia University Forum,* II, No. 2 (Fall 1958), 36.
[11] Lester B. Pearson, "Diplomacy in the Nuclear Age," *Foreign Service Journal,* Feb. 1959, p. 6.

matic level. There is danger in a process which leads men to think that nothing of importance can be settled except personally by the highest officials at the summit. It robs diplomacy of subtlety of maneuver based on extensive informal contacts through ambassadors engaged overtime in pointless or hypothetical talk—"If we do this, will you do that?" etc. But more important still, if the chief minister is continuously on the wing from Karachi to Paris to Manila, a vacuum grows up at the center at the point where larger policies must be evolved. If no one remains in Washington continually in personal touch with the dozens of issues that call for decision, then inevitably leadership and adaption become the high-priced casualty of personal diplomacy. In point of fact the price may be a ship of state modern and marvelously appointed but without a captain at the helm.

If I may state as specifically and directly as I can the dilemma of present-day diplomacy, it is this: Neither public nor personal diplomacy are by themselves adequate to the task, yet both are probably a permanent part of the present international landscape. They are in fact at opposite poles of a spectrum. One emphasizes public speeches, mass assemblies, and resolutions emerging from open forums; the other stresses informality and man-to-man conferences free of protocol, agendas, and advanced preparation. (At White Sulphur Springs in 1957 the Canadians on the eve of a Canadian-American "Little Summit" Conference did not know the topics to be discussed.) Yet these novel patterns, so divergent in conception and design, share one thing in common. Both public and personal diplomacy constitute a revolt against traditional diplomacy. They are "the new diplomacy."

The doubts men have about personal diplomacy stem in large part from a single source. The first rule of diplomacy has always been that negotiations were essential when national interests came into conflict. Since conflicts arise from causes more basic than personal hostility, personal amiability by itself can hardly resolve them. Sir Harold Nicolson has argued: "Diplomacy is the art of negotiating documents in a ratifiable and dependable form. It is by no means the art of conversation. The affability inseparable from any conversation . . . produces illusiveness, compromises and high intentions. Diplomacy if it is ever to be effective, should be a disagreeable business, and one recorded in hard print."

The trouble with personal diplomacy must be found in deep-seated philosophical roots that are reflected in the spirit of American foreign relations. In social matters most approaches are either too ready to set aside the lessons of the past or alternatively are not prepared to see the present in all its complexity, novelty, and richness. Any agreement if it comes in the cold war will almost certainly be the product of long, tedious, even agonizing preparation by professional diplomats including those like Ambassador Llewelyn Thompson in constant touch with the pulse of policy-making in Moscow. The Austrian Peace Treaty will be a case study for years to come of a settlement based on long and arduous diplomatic preparation. However, it is also true that powers of decision in Russia, Britain, France, and Germany have increasingly gravitated toward the summit of government. Not Foreign Secretaries but Prime Ministers hold in their hands authority to accept proposals, make concessions, and ameliorate the dread struggle in which the world is gripped. Thus our contemporaries who see in personal diplomacy the key to world peace are correct but so are those who stress preparations at appropriate diplomatic levels. Somehow these two approaches must be blended in modern diplomacy if civilization is to survive.

All the issues implicit in the dilemma of modern diplomacy come to a focus in the present conflict over Berlin. It is issues like these with which modern techniques must cope. Russian intentions here remain as in the past a riddle wrapped in mystery inside an enigma which may remain unfathomable even to modern diplomacy at its best. Yet the West still has within its grasp the possibility, however slender and fleeting, of discovering answers to questions such as these: Would the Russians be prepared to guarantee the permanent status of a free city of both West and East Berlin in return for recognition of the sovereignty of East Germany? What price are Soviet leaders prepared to pay for a denuclearized Central Europe in which neither West Germany, East Germany, Czechoslovakia, or Poland would be given thermonuclear weapons? What about the thinning out as well of conventional forces or at least a freezing of present levels of force as a part of some form of disengagement? If Western observers looking to the triumph of socialist regimes in Germany and Britain are correct in predicting the inevitable withdrawal of Western troops from Germany and perhaps all Europe, can we negotiate now a more limited withdrawal at the price of commitments from the Russians? Are there ways that outstanding issues can be joined together or packaged in some fashion to achieve a result that both sides find disagreeable at certain points but sufficiently palatable in the end to furnish a basis for working things out? Do Khrushchev's need for an internal political victory and his continuing difficulties in the satellite states plus the fear of German nuclear rearmament point to a stimulus and a formula for discussion? Might a European Security System be worked out grounded in the U.N. but explicitly addressed to these fears? Might the threat of an aggressive, expansionist China on the east and a rising Germany harnessed to the power and resources of NATO in the west prompt the Russians to make concessions as Khrushchev has hinted in talks with Adlai Stevenson, Walter Lippmann, and Senator Humphrey? Are Soviet interests in an over-all European settlement of an order to lend credence to Winston Churchill's counsel: "It is idle to reason or argue with the Communists. It is, however, possible to deal with them on a fair, realistic basis and, in my experience, they will keep their bargains as long as it is in their interest to do so, which might in this grave matter, be a long time, once things were settled." Do all sides for whom peace hangs precariously on "a balance of terror" have common interests in treating the cancerous situation in Central Europe?

No reasonable man can believe that this offer or that proposal by itself would lead to a *detente*. Nor should anyone imagine that improved diplomatic procedures are in themselves any panacea. We must recognize, first of all, our present weakness, especially in Berlin, where for the present standing firm and perhaps mounting a new airlift may be the best we can do. However if the United States has no more than force and new strategic doctrines to offer, opinion in Western Europe can hardly be expected to follow our leadership particularly in the long run. There is an intricate relation between the seriousness of provocation and the firm measures for which support may be gained. Merely technical changes by the Communists including giving the East Germans authority to stamp documents on traffic into West Berlin will not bring world opinion to the support of far-reaching acts of force. Moreover, Soviet leaders enjoy all the advantages of conducting negotiations in the "normal way." They can put out extreme terms and bargain down to their minimum interests. In the West both those in and out of government face the censure of free opinion in shaping a negotiating position in these terms. However, the horrendous consequences that threaten the world if there are no negotiations make the formulation of excessive but negotiable demands as essential as they are painful and almost certainly unpopular.

Yet significantly even if America stood alone or if the dilemmas of democratic and public diplomacy were less far-reaching, the task in the present crisis would be much the same. America's call to greatness would require unmatched vigor and public courage in resolving to organize and prepare the sinews of military strength. However, the chances of survival in peace or in a thermonuclear struggle require something more than a national resolve to be firm and strong. There is need as well for eternal vigilance in seeking out reasonable prospects for accommodation in the cold war. The watchword in diplomacy is "the best is often the enemy of the good." The best opportunity for a political solution is one which may never come. An awareness of this is perhaps the sole means of rising above and escaping the final dilemma in foreign policy.

Chapter Three

JUDAEO-CHRISTIAN REALISM: THE COLD WAR AND THE SEARCH FOR RELEVANT NORMS

> "There have accumulated around the Christian tradition various forms of worldly wisdom which condense the experience of centuries and have come to stand as part of our European heritage."—HERBERT BUTTERFIELD

With the present subject I come to the heart of the problem of ethics and foreign policy. For men and states, the search for justice and morality, whether in Augustine or in Plato or with contemporary writers, is a bewildering, frustrating, and uncertain task. Perhaps for this reason modern man is disposed to set it aside for more limited and manageable types of inquiry. Why not assume, in economics for instance, the model of an "economic man" who can be analyzed and appraised as if man's one goal was the maximization of profit? Or, alternatively, in things political, the assumption that all men seek power appears for many writers to be a more orderly and rational measure of political behavior. In the era of vastness and complexity through which civilization is presently dog-paddling, the insistence that we exclude the ethical and religious component appears virtually overpowering. I suggest we consider five attempts to come to terms with the relevance of ethical norms in three areas in which the problem is particularly acute.

1. *The Problem of Relevant Norms in Economics, History, and Diplomacy*

Even those students of economic and political life who concede that religion has some contribution to make are profoundly impressed with the difficulties. For example, John Maurice Clark, a contributor to the economic studies of the National Council of Churches, writes: "Religion starts with values so pure that they are likely to seem inapplicable in any political and economic life except one for which an earthy humanity is not yet ready. And if one tries to carry out some of these values in the world of politics, business, or trade unions, one faces the necessity of marginal adjustments between values of different sorts. But because these values have been presented as absolutes, not subject to compromise, the individual finds himself convicted of inevitable sin, no matter how selfless his motives and how clear his understanding, because, forsooth, he is acting like economic man and weighing marginal increments of different kinds of values against one another." [1] Professor Clark, therefore, maintains that only a marriage of technical competence and religious insight can yield a meaningful ethic for economics. Only someone who grasps both economic realities and the character of norms will have a contribution to make.

The controversy over morality in general and the moral evaluation of social action in particular also rages among students of contemporary history. Geoffrey Barraclough in his Stevenson Inaugural Lecture delivered at Chatham House on October 8, 1957, chose to discuss "History, Morals, and Politics." [2] He observed that not many years ago historians

---

[1] John Maurice Clark, *Economic Institutions and Human Welfare* (New York: Alfred A. Knopf, 1957), pp. 35–36.

[2] Geoffrey Barraclough, "History, Morals, and Politics," *International Affairs,* XXXIV, No. 1 (Jan. 1958), 1–15.

seemed to agree that their function was "to describe and explain, not to pronounce verdicts." The historian was not a judge but a detective who left any moral conclusions to his readers and their imaginations. With our recent unhappy experiences of unspeakably brutal tyrannies, totalitarian persecution, slave labor and concentration camps, this climate of opinion has noticeably shifted. In the words of Professor Barraclough's predecessor, Arnold J. Toynbee: "A historian is bound to make moral judgments on the human acts he is recording. . . . he could avoid making moral judgments only by closing his mind to the meaning of the story." [3] However, in the interests of clarity, Barraclough in his Inaugural insists that Mr. Toynbee's attitude must be subjected to critical scrutiny.

He asks, first of all, what of moral judgments in the field of private morality? Does it really add to the story to denounce in explicit terms the "wicked" and "evil" private lives of monarchs like Henry II or Emperor Charles the Great, or "the savage crimes" of Cromwell? When one condemns Charles the Great and Cromwell for their wickedness, what have we gained? "Are we supposed to strip off their title to greatness, like the decorations from a cashiered officer? Are we to do a subtraction sum from their major, admitted, positive achievements, and precisely how do we strike the balance?" Barraclough maintains that the question of moral judgment is more complicated than it is fashionable to admit. The gist of his argument is stated in these words:

I would not suggest that the moral issue is irrelevant, and certainly nothing should be suppressed; but it is only one issue among many, and I cannot easily believe it is the most important of those with which historians have to deal. For the historian is concerned, after all, mainly with consequences; and though the consequences of Cromwell's massacres in Ireland were an enduring legacy of Anglo-Irish animosity, the consequences of Charlemagne's massacres in Saxony were, curiously enough, the

[3] Quoted in *ibid.,* p. 4.

opposite; the Saxons were soon the most loyal supporters of the Frankish monarchy. In some ways, it almost seems, our moral judgments raise more problems than they solve; for, though it would be pleasant to think that nemesis always overtakes the evil-doer, if we are really honest, we shall have to ask whether, po-litically, evil does not sometimes pay. . . . In fact, whether we like it or not, [there are] two standards of morality, public or private. No one will suppose [this problem] . . . can be solved by the simple device of declaring that it does "violence to the basic notions of our morality." Of course it does: precisely that is "the problem of morality in history and politics." [4]

Professor Barraclough multiplies present-day examples to illustrate the complexity of moral judgment. President Nasser of Egypt is said by many in the West to have broken engage-ments freely entered into with British representatives. But "can we expect the Eastern peoples to share without question our attitude toward the inviolability of treaties . . . between a weak Eastern and a strong Western power?" "Further-more, although it is easy to argue that in changed circum-stances, a treaty freely negotiated should not be repudiated, but should be altered . . . by negotiation . . . this is more easily said than done. Instances do not come readily to mind, at least in cases where major political interests and national prestige are involved." [5] Insistence upon the inviolability of treaties is almost necessarily advantageous to those whom historians describe as "the beneficiaries of the status quo." Professor Barraclough concludes: "The brutal fact is that few young peoples would have secured their independence and their power to guide their own destiny if they had not broken through the network of public law constructed by the beneficiaries of the status quo to stabilize a position favourable to themselves; and few historians will be found to condemn them out of hand for this." [6]

But what of internal opponents of an existing political

[4] *Ibid.,* p. 6.
[5] *Ibid.,* p. 9.
[6] *Ibid.,* p. 10.

order? "We speak of people in Cyprus and Algeria as 'terrorists,' and our very choice of terms implies a moral judgment; but who, in fact, is the terrorist in Cyprus, Colonel Grivas, as perhaps 40 million English people think, or Colonel Harding, as perhaps 500 million Greeks, Africans and Indians think?" "As a Swiss commentator has pointed out, if the Algerians are 'terrorists,' so for the house of Hapsburg in the thirteenth century was William Tell." [7]

Barraclough finds the one residual sphere of practical morality for both historians and statesmen—and this is a point to which we shall return—in the ability to confront political reality on its own terms. To illustrate his concept, the Stevenson Professor chooses the controversy in an emergent German state between General von Gerlach and Prince Bismarck in the middle of the nineteenth century. Then, revolutionary France occupied the position Soviet Russia does today. In a debate of obvious contemporaneity, Gerlach charged Bismarck with failure to base his policy on opposition to the "evil spirit" of the Revolution in much the way that some contemporaries call for a holy war against Communism. He condemned "all political combinations as faulty, unsafe, and highly dangerous" when it came to courses of action in this profound moral struggle. Bismarck rejected Gerlach's approach, saying that to import such notions into politics was a surrender to "sympathies and antipathies." His ideal was "the habit of deciding independently of any feelings of antipathy to or preference for foreign states and their rulers." "The moral conception for which Gerlach stood —a conception which many today unconsciously echo—implies an abstract, transcendent, ethical norm, an extraneous principle by which everything else is judged and which retains its imperative quality without reference to the fact whether or not it can be translated into political practice. For Bismarck, on the contrary, morality is not an abstract

[7] *Ibid.*

conception standing outside political reality, but stems from within it; it is concrete and immanent, and is expressed in the statesman's sense of moral responsibility for his actions." [8] This viewpoint frees the statesmen from the beckoning will-of-the-wisp of moral crusades against evil which eventuate so often in strident calls for preventive wars. In Bismarck's words: "A statesman cannot create anything himself; he must wait and listen until he hears the steps of God sounding through events and then leap up and grasp the hem of his garment." [9] On the eve of the Austro-Prussian War of 1866, he warned those who would punish Austria for its wickedness: "Austria was no more wrong in opposing our claims than we were in making them." [10] Barraclough posits this as a relevant morality for the West in the cold war.

Herbert Butterfield, the Cambridge historian and Master of Peterhouse, has analyzed international morality and the historical process in a series of important writings and his conclusions, though similar, are fundamentally different from Barraclough's. The most characteristic statement of his viewpoint appears in books like *Christianity, War and Diplomacy; Christianity and History* and *Christianity and European History*. Morality, in his view, is not one thing for the statesman and another thing for the rest of mankind. There is no such thing as a separate political ethic. Philosophers and poets, no less than decision-makers, must daily choose not between good and evil but between lesser evils or partial goods. The quality of the decision, fundamentally at least, is the same whether in politics or business, education or family life. Therefore Butterfield has argued: "I don't see why in politics the virtues which I associate with the Christian religion should be suspended: humility, charity, self-judgment, and acceptance of the problem Providence sets

[8] *Ibid.*, p. 14.
[9] A. J. P. Taylor, *Bismarck, The Man and the Statesman* (New York: Knopf, 1955), p. 115.
[10] *Ibid.*, p. 87.

before one; also a disposition not to direct affairs as a sovereign will in the world, but to make one's action a form of co-operation with Providence." [11]

Professor Butterfield grounds his conception of international morality in three general propositions. First, morality, as he conceives it, derives ultimately from a "higher law" espoused alike by "lapsed Christians" and religious thinkers according to which nothing but human beings exist or matter. Second, morality must be sharply distinguished from every form of moralistic program and creed which, embodied in a crusade, would claim for its partial insights a more ultimate standing than they deserve. Third, an international order exists as the ultimately relevant objective standard against which national interests must be measured.

The first proposition prompts Professor Butterfield to insist that the social order requires men who would preserve themselves and their values to have "respect for the other man's personality, the other man's end. . . ." [12] In a word, men in the final analysis live in a moral order, however ambiguous its particular forms and expressions may be. Present-day thought has difficulty with this conception for, on the one hand, liberal philosophies which accept as their sole premise the "rights of man" run the risk of encouraging an unbridled egotism according to which man need obey the law only if he agrees with it. On the other hand, thinking which starts with the "duties of man" is likely to end by making him the slave of the state. That is why both man and the state must be subject to a transcendent moral and political order which prompts them to treat one another as more than means to an end. In this connection, "if in the Anglo-Saxon world there has been the necessary amount of the spirit of give-and-take, the disposition to compromise, respect

[11] Herbert Butterfield, "Morality and Historical Process in International Affairs," unpublished manuscript for June 12, 1956, meeting of Columbia University Seminar on Theory of International Politics, p. 1.
[12] *Ibid.*, p. 2.

for the other man's opinion and the reluctance to resort to desperation-policies," [13] this may be due to our greater security, our longer political experience or our state of urbanity free from violence; but it may also be due to the survival of religious influences. We are members of a single Western civilization or cultural community which embraces the moral criteria of the Judaeo-Christian tradition. In some communities, the absence of "a higher law" or regulative principle makes for doctrinaire politics, and "those who have no religion are particularly liable to bring a religious fanaticism to problems of mundane organization which ought to be matters for transaction and negotiation. Lord Acton was probably right when he said that liberty is impossible except amongst people who have a sense that the whole political game is being played in a realm over which there rules a higher law." [14]

If the beginning of wisdom is the recognition that men live finally in some kind of a moral order, the next step is an awareness that the moral is not merely moralistic. Moral judgments can sometimes be used to conceal practical responsibilities from society and from oneself. "A careless librarian, who establishes no regular system for the checking of his books may be satisfied just to heap blame on the people whose delinquencies have resulted in gaps in his shelves." [15] His pious preachments against dishonesty and in favor of virtue can hardly excuse his lack of responsibility. Moreover, moral judgments may also spill over into Pharisaism, exemplified by the priggish moralizers Christ condemned in the Gospels. If there are obscurities in the Gospels, this text is not among them. Nothing is clearer than the distinction between those who claim to be and those who are righteous. We recall the parable of the Pharisee and the publican in the Gospel according to St. Luke.

[13] *Ibid.*
[14] *Ibid.*
[15] *Ibid.*, p. 3.

The moral lesson to be drawn from this parable is not that some states are pharisaic and others truly righteous, but rather that all nations are strongly disposed to endow their particular national ethical systems with universal validity. Nations find themselves today in a situation not too dissimilar from that obtaining domestically within the United States prior to the Civil War. The sanctities of religion and science are invoked to show that one course of action, one nation's program, will execute a divine mandate. Nations go to war not in dispute over territorial boundaries but to make the world safe for democracy or to destroy human wickedness incarnated in evil men like Hitler and Mussolini. Wars of righteousness in which compromise and limited objectives are looked on as treason are today's counterpart of earlier historical wars of religion.

Professor Butterfield's diagnosis of the present crisis brings him to offer some practical alternatives. He finds that "once the aggressor is held in check, and once a balance of forces is achieved, the healing processes of time, and these alone, can solve our problem. . . ." [16] The core of his prescription for peace and morality, therefore, is time and the absence of war and revolution. Any conflict that time and reason cannot solve will not be solved by war. He is persuaded that it is possible to live with ideological deadlocks and to discover a *modus vivendi,* as in the struggle between Catholicism and Protestantism, and Islam and Christianity. With patience and good luck, justice can eventually emerge. His critics ask whether this is not a counsel of perfection. How would this precept have applied to Hitler? Apparently Butterfield believes that a balance of forces against Hitler sometime prior to 1939 might have prevented the conflict and allowed time to work its healing effect.

A more general alternative to wars of righteousness is a restoration of the international order. "On moral grounds,

[16] *Ibid.*

as well as on prudential calculations, national egotism requires to be checked, superseded and transcended." [17] Partly this demands "every possible variation and extension of the art of putting oneself—and actually feeling oneself—in the other person's (or nation's) place." [18] It requires states to recognize themselves as imperfect parts of an imperfectly ethical world and to show a somewhat greater awareness of the moral complexities and disparities in the objective environment underlying the state behavior of others. Beyond this, statesmen must ask the question whether their policies are likely to produce the kind of international order in which their own values can survive. In this sense they transcend national self-interest at the point of the query, "Everything considered, what is best for the world?" Indeed "a state may fairly acquire virtue from the very fact that it contrives to make its self-interest harmonize with something that is good for the world in general." [19] A case in point may be the liquidation of large segments of the British Empire when morality and the necessity of reducing its overseas commitments converged in a common policy. In this same connection, the intrinsic logic of the Marshall Plan comes naturally to mind. In Mr. Butterfield's words: "Whether we are practising diplomacy, or conducting a war, or negotiating a peace treaty, our ultimate objective is the maintenance and the development of an international order. This is the purpose which transcends national egotism and puts the boundary to self-interest—the purpose to which all our more immediate aims in foreign policy have reference." [20]

Two exceedingly able American diplomatists—former Sec-

---

[17] *Ibid.*, p. 10.
[18] Professor Butterfield distinguishes between the moralist and the statesman in this way: "The moralist and the teacher, the prophet and the preacher, address themselves to the improvement of human nature itself. . . . The statesman is concerned to improve human conduct rather by the process of rectifying conditions." *Ibid.*, pp. 8–9.
[19] *Ibid.*, p. 10.
[20] *Ibid.*, p. 11.

retary of State Dean Acheson and onetime Director of the Policy Planning Staff George F. Kennan—have each undertaken to define the place of morality and religion in international politics. Both share with historians like Barraclough and Butterfield a profound uneasiness over the prevailing trend toward national self-righteousness where every practical measure is cloaked in the garb of moral and political virtue. In Mr. Acheson's telling phrase: "To express collective indignation may bring the glow of moral principles vindicated without effort; but it is usually futile, and, more often than not, harmful." [21] We must be careful not to pose "as the schoolmistress of the Western hemisphere." [22] Both men are hesitant to "use the language of moral discourse," preferring instead to describe foreign policy in terms of purpose and effect. They are reluctant to introduce the distinctions of moral and immoral as descriptions of state behavior, because "the language of moral discourse—colored as it is apt to be at one end with fervor, and, at the other, with self-righteousness—is more likely to obscure than to clarify. . . ." [23] For this reason both men strike out against what they call "the moralistic-ideological" approach.

If I read them correctly, they mean by this the tendency of "finding in one theme both a central evil, which is thought to dominate our time, and also the clue to its eradication." [24] Such a theme oftentimes amounts to reducing moral principles to maxims which are easily corrupted into slogans. Such a theme I have already discussed in what has been said about "the dilemma of colonialism." According to Mr. Acheson, a moralistic approach to the colonial problem insists "that not only do communities which wish to break off existing political connections and become independent na-

[21] Dean Acheson, *Power and Diplomacy* (Cambridge, Massachusetts: Harvard University Press, 1958), p. 80.
[22] *Ibid.*
[23] *Ibid.*, p. 108.
[24] Dean Acheson, "Morality, Moralism and Diplomacy," *The Yale Review*, XLVII, No. 4 (June 1958), 485.

tional states have a moral right to do so, but that a moral
foreign policy on the part of the United States requires that
we go to considerable lengths to help them, including the
use of force. . . ." [25] This principle, whether we call it support of popular revolutionary movements or self-determination, was applied enthusiastically against our enemies in
two world wars, particularly in the dismemberment of the
Austro-Hungarian and Ottoman Empires. However, "as one
looks back upon the results in Eastern Europe and the Middle East, one has more difficulty in seeing the moral or ideal
achievement than in recognizing the immediate end, perhaps, irrevocable disaster." [26] The problem becomes most
acute when we deal with states that are politically more in-
transigent and resistant. The cases of India in Kashmir,
Hungary, and the Baltic states come quickly to mind. In
cases such as these, policy-makers ironically enough tend to
shift the invocation of the principle in order to apply it
boldly—perhaps in remission of failures elsewhere—to the
problems of our friends. Mr. Acheson is brutally non-partisan
in leveling this criticism at Senator Kennedy for his preachments directed toward the French. The single-factor approach, whether its object lies in Senator McCarthy's threat
of Communists in government, or President Eisenhower's
peril of Communist imperialism, or Senator Kennedy's end
of colonialism partakes of an illusory simplicity. It carries
within it, however, serious pitfalls and traps. If Communism
is the sole threat, we run the risk of making dyed-in-the-wool
crusaders against Communism who historically have been
demoniac figures like Hitler or Mussolini, or shadowy leaders
like Franco, our staunchest co-workers in building resistance
to Communist expansionism. The gravest peril lies in being
driven to embrace allies because of what they oppose, not
because of what they propose.

[25] *Ibid.*, p. 483.
[26] *Ibid.*

Under such circumstances, it would be better to adopt a strategic rather than a moralistic approach. The spirit of this approach is reflected in Bret Harte's "Tennessee's Partner." "In fact, he was a grave man, with a steady application to practical detail which was unpleasant in difficulty." [27] Lincoln was denounced for immorality alike by abolitionists and secessionists, but for Mr. Acheson, Lincoln's dedication to the supreme goal of preserving the Union remains the classic embodiment of the strategic approach. Many of our contemporaries appraising the "Great Emancipator" overlook his epic statement in the letter he wrote to Horace Greeley on August 22, 1862:

My paramount objective is to save the Union, and is not either to save or destroy slavery. If I could save the Union without freeing any slave, I would do it; and if I could save it by freeing all the slaves, I would do it; and if I could do it by freeing some and leaving others alone, I would also do that. What I do about slavery and the colored race, I do because I believe it helps to save this Union; and what I forebear, I forebear because I do not believe it would help to save the Union. I shall do less whenever I shall believe what I am doing hurts the cause, and I shall do more whenever I shall believe doing more will help the cause.

Any moral choice involves decisions in a complicated and ever-shifting field of action. The same course of action that under one set of circumstances may be moral, in another may be quite immoral. To sort out the moral elements in each successive crisis is the task of statesmanship, and simple moralism is more often an impediment than a guide.

In more general philosophic terms, Mr. Kennan believes there are few if any absolutes in international politics. When one considers Kennan's viewpoint, one thinks of Lord Acton's counsel: "An absolute principle is as absurd as absolute power," or his advice: "When you perceive a truth, look for the balancing truth." Such a philosophy is singularly

[27] Quoted in *ibid.*, p. 487.

appropriate in foreign policy, for when our diplomats and statesmen are dealing with a foreign country their role is, at best, a marginal one. They can help or encourage existing or latent tendencies on foreign soil, but it is for those more intimately responsible for another country's affairs to realize them. Needless to say, this runs counter to certain basic American emotions. It is tempting to proclaim that this troubled world could be free of all conflict if only peoples everywhere would adopt the political institutions we have forged in the fire of national experience. "The Wilsonian thesis was . . . that, since the world was no longer safe for the American democracy, the American people were called upon to conduct a crusade to make the world safe for American democracy. In order to do this the principles of the American democracy would have to be made universal throughout the world." [28]

However, there is no absolutely best state for all peoples. We are reminded of de Tocqueville's words on the United States written in 1831: "The more I see of this country the more I admit myself penetrated with this truth: that there is nothing absolute in the theoretical value of political institutions, and that their efficiency depends almost always on the original circumstances and the social conditions of people to whom they are applied." The ways in which peoples move toward more enlightened forms of government constitute the most profound of the processes of national life. They stem from the bedrock of national character and existence; they have an organic growth. For example, Kennan, writing on the subject "When the Russians Rose Against the Czar," concludes by saying that if changes were to take place in the Soviet Union, Americans would do well "not to impede or embarrass the process by claiming it for our own and by attempting to see in it the repetition and vindication, in

[28] Walter Lippmann, *Isolation and Alliances: An American Speaks to the British* (Boston: Little Brown & Co., 1952), p. 22.

universal terms, of our own history. It is her own laws of development, not ours, that Russia must follow. The sooner we learn that there are many mansions in this house of nations, and many paths to the enrichment of human experience, the easier we will make it for other people to solve their problems, and for ourselves to understand our own." [29] In stressing this point it is barely possible that Mr. Kennan has neglected the corollary that notwithstanding endless variations there are minimum standards of justice and order that any polity must observe lest the fabric of mankind be threatened. It may be that some of the classical writers were more attuned to this problem than the children of our present relativist age. Classicists were ever in search of the attributes of the best state, however transcendent these might be.

Mr. Kennan and his school of policy planners has also resisted a too absolute conception of the possible goals and accomplishments of foreign policy. It is well to be ever aware of the limits as well as the purposes of foreign policy, the boundaries as well as the magnitudes. The statesman confronting the world is constrained, more often than not, to act within narrow limits. His choices are severely restricted and events pass swiftly beyond the realm of conscious choice. Oftentimes he faces a moral predicament of an almost insoluble character. Such a predicament seems to be presented by World War II, for its roots are embedded fatefully and inextricably in the aftermath of World War I. France and England had been weakened far more deeply than they knew. Austria-Hungary had disappeared as a restraint on Germany. Russia was no longer a predictable and constructive force, for it had been seized by violent men who were implacably hostile to those capitalist societies to which political necessity might have united them as natural allies. Into this setting marched the one great united people in Central Europe,

[29] *New York Times Magazine*, March 10, 1957, p. 40.

the Germans—"frustrated, impoverished, stung with defeat, uncertain in the breakdown of their traditional institutions." In the light of these facts it is all too easy to absolve Western statesmen of any responsibility and to regard them as "actors in a tragedy beyond their making or repair." [30]

While the choices of Western statesmen were significantly and tragically narrowed by this tangled web of events and nothing approaching a complete solution was to be found, possibilities of making wiser and more effectual choices were never entirely eliminated. For example, it might have been possible to lend greater encouragement, support, and understanding to certain moderate forces within the Weimar Republic. A different attitude toward the defeated German people, "one less dominated by distaste, suspicion and social snobbery," might have strengthened the more liberal forces which were not totally lacking in Germany at that time. And once the struggle seemed inevitable the West might have deterred it—especially in 1936 at the time of the occupation of the Rhineland—by a firm show of strength, or later by a resolute military build-up that even tyrannies would have had to respect. At last, when war came, the allies could have made a decisive stand not for total victory but for more limited military and political objectives sometimes possible in war.

Finally, Kennan and Acheson, while admitting that individual and collective morality have something in common, are fearful of analogies that treat the two as more or less identical. "Generally speaking, morality . . . imposes upon those who exercise the powers of government a standard of conduct quite different from what might seem right to them as private citizens." [31] The moral rights and duties of the judge is not to do what he thinks right or, by his judicial action, to recast society in terms more appropriate, say, to his

[30] George F. Kennan, *American Diplomacy, 1900–1950* (Chicago: University of Chicago Press, 1951), p. 78.
[31] Acheson, "Morality and Diplomacy," p. 489.

vision of the justice of natural law. "It is our hope that the consciences of our judges will be guided, not by what they think is right, but what they believe the law requires them to decide, whether they like it or not." [32] Similarly, the pursuit of personal advantage or the service of special interests or groups, while commonly accepted in private life, has no legitimate place in public service. Indeed, a whole network of conflict-of-interest laws has been thrown up for government servants to guard them against vulnerability to private pressures.

Governments exist primarily to maintain order and justice within certain territorial boundaries and provide at the same time for the common defense. Neither the domestic nor international purposes of the state strictly coincide with Christian principles or the will of God. The function of the state is rather to protect man from himself—his greed, lust, and brutality. This is a worthy function, but one required less for Christian purposes than because men are less than Christian in conduct. The state being an agent and not a principal, a collectivity rather than an individual, is incapable of assuming the personal or subjective obligations that inhere in the concept of Christian justice. In Mr. Kennan's words: "Christian justice is a two way street, in that it implies an obligation of charity and humility and sacrifice on the dispenser of justice as well as on its object. The father's treatment of the prodigal son was founded on a Christian recognition of the relevance to this situation not just of the son's delinquency but also of the father's own sin and guilt. But our secular father, the state, is incapable of making any such recognition. It is always guiltless in its own eyes. Its justice, accordingly, remains and must remain—less than Christian." [33] Relations among states are even more infected with this less than

[32] Ibid.
[33] The following quotations are taken from an address by Mr. Kennan to the students and faculty of Princeton Theological Seminary in the winter of 1959, subsequently published as "Foreign Policy and Christian Conscience," *The Atlantic Monthly*, CCIII, No. 5 (May 1959), 44-49.

Christian quality. "Nowhere in Christ's teachings," Mr. Kennan argues, "was it suggested that mankind ought to be divided into political families . . . [of sovereign states], each a law unto itself, each recognizing no higher authority than its own national ego, each assuming its interest to be more worthy of service than any other with which it might come into conflict. . . . Before we could talk about a wholly Christian foreign policy, we would have to overcome this unlimited egoism of the sovereign national state and find a higher interest which all of us could recognize and serve."

Christian moralists and utopian rationalists interestingly enough are seized by the same illusion. It was comparatively simple for a brilliant essayist like Bertrand Russell in his exchanges in the *New Statesman* with Premier Khrushchev and Secretary Dulles last winter to point out contradictions. He noted that both believe in progress but both maintain that it will depend on adoption of their respective social systems even to the extent of preparing for nuclear war in defense of these goals. Yet nuclear war would mean mutual destruction and Lord Russell therefore called for full and free rational debate to establish the truth and bring a lessening in the acerbity of the East-West ideological struggle. At present, both accuse the other's system of every kind of vice, claiming for their own every virtue. Lord Russell tended to argue that competing ideologies, like scientific theories, must be debated by appeal to fact and logic and modified when circumstances require. However, a nation's political ideals are the cement by which a society is united and consolidated against the external world. Through them statesmen fuse the multifarious pressures that compose society into coherent lines of action. They are the means of concerting the national will; they represent everything about their people in a favorable light. Their function is not, as in science, to explain events but to assemble a vast miscellany of popular feelings and bring it to the point of action. It is illusory to imagine that such points of political doctrine can be judged and corrected by higher moral or rational standards or debated out of existence. The best we can hope is that if the people achieve a certain skepticism about the more absolute claims, their statesmen will reflect this when they come to the conference table and will fix more on the practical points in a settlement than scoring points in ideological war.

Mr. Kennan concludes: "All these reflections cause me to wince when I hear people confusing the possibilities and obligations of the state with the possibilities and obligations of the Christian individual. . . . I wince . . . when I hear it claimed that the foreign policy of our own government has already achieved so remarkable a state of innocence and purity of motive as to justify us in regarding it as a religious crusade and in giving it devotion and support in this quality." "To the extent that the Kingdom of God is to be realized at all on this earth, it is going to be realized in the human heart: in the struggle of the individual against the powers of darkness within himself, in his transcendence of instinctive self-will, . . . in his elevation of mind and spirit to that level of detachment and of compassionate identification with others which we know as Christian love. It is not to be realized in the workings of the state, with its imperfect justice, its pretense to moral infallibility, its purely external enemies, and its absurd claim to be a law and a purpose unto itself." [34]

Yet Kennan is constrained to urge that no one equate his viewpoint with a counsel of despair on the workings of sovereign states or an advocacy of quietism, passivity, or indifference for the Christian as he confronts the real world. The state "cannot assure the triumph of Christian love, but it can do things that affect the possibilities for its advancement." It can provide a decent human environment in which man can work out his destiny, and whether he suc-

[34] *Ibid.*

ceeds in realizing this is singularly dependent on the individual's response to his responsibilities of citizenship and public duty. Mr. Kennan sees "no way in which we can absolve ourselves of our tiny individual share of responsibility for what the government does." That the state has immense possibilities for evil is all too plain from Nazi Germany, the Soviet Union, and Communist China, where the most appalling lines of cruelty have fostered "a real sickness of the human spirit . . . dreadfully adverse to . . . the Christian cause." However, the state also enjoys vast possibilities for good if the body politic be healthy, vital, and alert to international issues which may have significance from the Christian standpoint.

Mr. Kennan maintains that questions of method in foreign policy are generally the ones best suited to Christian concern as against questions of purpose which tend to be broadly determined by basic underlying forces. The latter involve such issues as a statesman's intent and all the excruciatingly complex relationships between a man's or government's aims and the consequences of action. In so far as methods go, "a government can pursue its purposes in a patient and conciliatory and understanding way, respecting the interests of others and infusing its behavior with a high standard of decency and honesty and humanity, or it can show itself petty, exacting, onerous, and self-righteous." Good purposes will be undermined by dubious methods "whereas sheer good manners will bring some measure of redemption to even the most ill-conceived and disastrous of undertakings." The Christian citizen, therefore, should focus his interest on a government's style and its methods of seeking its aims. "If we allow ourselves to copy our adversary's methods as a means of combatting, him, we may have lost the battle before we start. . . ." In the cold war, "while Christian values may be, and often are, involved in the issues of our conflict with Soviet power, we cannot conclude that everything we want automatically reflects the purpose of God and everything they want—the purpose of the Devil. The pattern is complex, fuzzy and unstable. We must bear in mind all the things we do not know and cannot know. We must concede, I think, the possibility that there might be some areas of conflict involved in this cold war which a Divine Power could contemplate only with a sense of pity and disgust for both parties, and others in which . . . He might even consider us wrong." [35]

2. The Limitations of the Judaeo-Christian Perspective

The red thread that runs through the broad outlines of thought expressed in the writings we have examined contains at least two important strands. Each of these extraordinary minds, from Professor Clark to Mr. Kennan, has stressed the limitations affecting any application of the Judaeo-Christian perspective to foreign policy while at the same time pointing to realms in which for them it achieves its most significance and relevance. I would propose now to make explicit, first, the limitations of the Christian perspective in foreign policy for the cold war and, secondly, its applicability or relevance in the realm of foreign affairs.

Today much of contemporary religious teaching and writing cannot conceal its impatience at the mere mention of limitations. The spokesmen for positive thinking, to the extent they deal at all with the great, burning questions of policy and action, would wish them away through incantations and appeals to God—each man's and each nation's favorite trouble shooter. They find as few occasions as possible to speak to the troublesome day-to-day problems with which less sanctified leaders continuously grapple. When they do speak, they choose to solve them with general prescriptions for piety and perfectionism. Thus America's most popular evangelist declares there would be no "Russian problem"

[35] *Ibid.*

if in the sprawling metropolis of New York Christians were to wipe out the twin evils of juvenile delinquency and prostitution. Or on another occasion, he proclaimed his doubts that pre-Communist-China could have suffered from public and private corruption since Chiang Kai-shek prayed to God several times a day. Sometimes Christians and non-Christians alike, faced with theologies of this kind that are so completely irrelevant to the pressing issues of the time, are tempted to join the refrain: "God save us from our friends." One thinks of the German scientist Hahn, who had above his desk a plaque which read: "God, help me to bear at least some of my own burdens without laying them all on Thee."

Yet there is a richer, more authentic and enduring Christian tradition free of all the illusions and confusions of the presently fashionable revivalist trend. From Augustine to Niebuhr, Christian realism at almost every point in time has sought to grapple patiently with the perplexities and limitations of the day. This tradition, I would suggest, is directly relevant to the search for applicable norms in the cold war and to a facing up to the limitations within which such norms must be operative.

The first limitation stems from the curiously ambiguous role the Church must play whenever it speaks on social issues. It stems in a word from the inevitable dualism of the Christian point of view. On the one hand, Christianity declares that because men have a touch of God within them, they cannot rest so long as suffering, injustice, and exploitation prevail. In an earlier day, John Milton wrote: "My conscience I have from God and I cannot give it to Caesar." According to this faith, men believe that the spirit of God gives the ultimate standards of social criticism. In early American life, religious convictions inspired men to enter the public forum to join the good fight. De Tocqueville sensed this when he wrote of the Americans of his day: "To take a hand in the regulation of society and to discuss it is his highest concern . . . if an American were condemned to confine his activities to his own affairs he would be robbed of one half of his existence."

Yet on the other hand, at the heart of much Christian thought lurks the counterview that Caesar's world and God's never meet. Surprisingly enough, John Foster Dulles asserted this doctrine more than once before his religious conversion in 1937–1938. In ancient Rome, Tertullian wrote: "We have for Caesar the image of Caesar which is impressed on the coin, for God, the image of God which is impressed on human beings. Give Caesar his money: give yourself to God." However, for Tertullian, giving himself to God was so all-consuming that he could boast: "I owe no obligation to forum, campus or senate. I stay awake for no public function. I make no effort to monopolize the platform. I pay no heed to any administrative duty." Doubtless, attitudes of social indifference such as this prompted Gibbon's charge that Christians preoccupied with otherworldliness and unwilling or unable to meet the day's problems paved the way for the downfall of Rome.

This limitation of course is more than ancient history. It expresses itself again today in the age-old question: Are religion and life a unity or must they inevitably go their separate ways? More particularly, are Christianity and our common national and international life related or do they perforce exist in separate, watertight compartments? Nearly every book in the spirit of Bertrand Russell's *Why I Am Not A Christian* assumes Christianity invariably chooses social and political isolation. Mr. Russell and his friends attack not the truth or falsity of Christianity but rather its essential irrelevance. In much the same vein, secular writers describing a fruitless international conference in which one pious, moralistic pronouncement follows another frequently compare it to the atmosphere of a church. Or Sidney Hyman,

discussing the advantages American governors enjoy as can-
didates for the presidency, especially in competition with
Senators who have taken clearcut positions on successive
national and international issues, concludes that governors
go to their party conclaves with far greater strength. "They
can enter a convention free, like a fashionable sermon, of
any repelling wrangle, tangle or angle." [36]

Religious men and women may be stung by such sug-
gestions. They do well to ask themselves, however, why it
is that intellectuals and ordinary Americans often find these
imputations at least partly convincing. One reason such
charges sometimes carry a plausible ring has roots in religion's tendency toward perfectionism whenever it invades
the realm of international affairs. Harold Nicolson, who is
probably the West's most articulate student of historic diplomacy, suggests that religious persons compared to cynics
make poor diplomats. He offers in explanation their tendency of forever talking about absolute principles in what is
essentially a practical art. One example of their state of mind
appears in the assertion that "if other men and nations were
Christian, there would be no war." Closer to home in more familiar matters, Christians rarely make these extravagant
claims. Thus who among us argues that if all men were Christian there would be no divorce? In the everyday world most
men take their private tragedies in stride. When misfortune
strikes, they recognize, at least in the quiet of their rooms,
that somehow they themselves are partly to blame. With
Paul, they acknowledge that a Christian's behavior is not
perfection, that Christianity even for the most saintly is a
process of becoming that ends only with the grave.

Nonetheless, the Christian spokesman for a nation, or even
the Christian citizen, has the greatest difficulty indulging
himself in this kind of humility and self-examination. His

[36] *New York Times Magazine,* Jan. 4, 1959, p. 47.

people demand that he be positive and claim new triumphs at every point along the way. The realm of foreign affairs is riddled through and through with choices of the most exceptional difficulty for every would-be Christian. In our personal lives, we take for granted, however sadly, the fact that human friendships will normally be temporary, guarded, and incomplete and that acts of generosity and kindness more often than not go unacknowledged. If this were not so, would we look back with deep nostalgia to the warm abandon of childhood friends or the close bonds that grew up among wartime comrades? Ironically enough in another sphere, Christians and non-Christians alike just as normally demand and expect gratitude from those who receive aid in foreign relations. We too easily forget that governments fall when they confess too openly their dependence on others. It seems fair to say that this factor was one cause of the fall in 1958 of a pro-Western government in Lebanon and perhaps in Iraq. In international relations there may be some truth in that harsh but ancient saying: "Do a man a good turn and he will never forgive you."

There is a second dilemma having to do with man and his conception of himself. Religion in its profoundest moments has not blinked at the truth set forth by an early Christian realist, St. Paul. His words ring true for political no less than personal relations: "For the good that I would not, it is no more I that do it, but sin that dwelleth in me. I find then a law, that, when I would do good, evil is present with me. For I delight in the law of God after the inward man: But I see another law in my members, warring against the law of my mind, and bringing me into captivity to the law of sin which is in my members." [37] This for Paul was the nature and source of the human predicament. The only escape for unredeemed man lay outside history. "Who shall

[37] Romans 7:19–23.

deliver me from the body of this death. I thank God through Jesus Christ our Lord." [38]

Prevailing secular philosophies and popular religious movements are at odds with the Pauline tradition and endlessly challenge it from rostrum and pulpit. Any viewpoint which stresses man's war against himself is anathema to them; it is an outpouring of pessimism and defeatism which cannot be tolerated in an age of positive thinking. Anyone who dwells too long and too seriously on man as his own most baffling problem is denounced as an enemy of progress. The two points at which modern critics find themselves most at odds with Pauline thought are, first, on the nature of the human problem and, secondly, on the prescription for dealing with the problem.

Indeed, much of Western thought and no small part of Western history is a dialogue between two contending conceptions of man. Recently the two most blatant attacks on the Judaeo-Christian view have been Nazism and Communism. Nazism accepted the religious diagnosis only to propose ways and means of changing it. It sought with the instruments of modern science to breed man's failings out of existence. The key to the human predicament was to be a superior race. Human frailties would yield to rational biological programs. The Nazi political physicians were to graft superior physical, moral and intellectual qualities on to an evolving higher human race. Such a process, to be sure, required sacrifices of the weak to the strong. It justified as necessary hygienic measures extirpating inferior men and women who happened in a Teutonic state to be predominantly non-Gentiles.

The Communist attack on the human problem is of a somewhat different order. It looks to improvements of one facet of the human problem as essential remedies for all others. Marxists reason that the economic order in the capi-

[38] Romans 7:24-25.

talist West leads to class struggle and to social injustice. Rectify this and the state and man's exploitation of man will inevitably wither away. No price is too great to achieve this end. It is societies which have no all-consuming purpose that are most to be pitied. When Winston S. Churchill, during World War II, pressed Stalin on the brutal annihilation of millions of Russian kulaks, Stalin's response was to ask for a comparable example of Western sacrifice to so high a purpose. He, like Communist leaders who went before and those who have come after him, was deeply contemptuous of the lack in bourgeois society of any single higher purpose to which all else was subordinated.

If Nazism and Communism had been the only sources of criticism of the Christian view, a study of Western social and political thought as it relates to the Christian tradition would have little to propose, for Marxism is a deeply ingrained faith lying beyond the reach of reason. However, Western and American thinkers no less are endlessly tempted to shift the problem from man's struggle against himself. The American environment in particular has been remarkably fertile in these views. For some the real struggle is against ignorance. If men can be brought to higher cultural levels, they will not war with one another. For example, the historian Buckle found Russia's tendency toward conflict not in any inborn aggressive tendencies or any fundamental human problem but rather because the Russians were culturally barbarians. Yet one may ask what we are to think of the Germans, whose culture was certainly not inferior to that of those they invaded. Another variant of this philosophy assumes that men are unreasonable because they do not know one another. Multiply cultural exchange and tourism and they will become more reasonable toward one another. Yet one may ask whether France's proximity to Germany and the many contacts between Frenchmen and Germans have made them any more reasonable. Or has the presence of Westerners in former colonial areas made them more hated or loved than, say, the Russians whose contacts with such peoples begin only after World War II? Does knowledge of the motives, aspirations, and qualities of another people lead as often to suspicion, contempt, and even hatred? Ought we not therefore to be cautious about panaceas that are rooted in cultural exchange?

The struggle of man against himself is also translated by some into a struggle against myriad personal and social devils. Only a handful of evil men stand in the pathway to Utopia. In assessing the cause of World War I, a Congressional Committee first believed that profit-hungry munition makers had entrapped the American people in a headlong rush to a war nobody wanted. Or Hitler, Mussolini, and Stalin were each in turn pictured as evil incarnate whose personal elimination would restore harmony and goodwill to the world. The Far East was lost to the traitorous behavior of a handful of pro-Communist spies in the Department of State while Russian scientific advances are accounted for by pointing to men like Klaus Fuchs, who dipped into rich American scientific treasures to give Russia all she knows. The political campaigns for righteousness that periodically sweep over the American landscape likewise assume that a few evil or negligent men are responsible for all corruption in government. If Americans can learn anything from history, the lesson of the climax of the 1952 "moral crusade" in President Eisenhower's defense of Sherman Adams cannot but be instructive. President Eisenhower finally stood his ground by replying to the accusers in that revealing phrase, "I need him."

The one thing these myriad events, propositions, and phenomena on the political landscape have in common is the attempt to erect a means of escaping from the fundamental human predicament. Deep and lasting problems are accounted for in simple institutional or personal terms. One single assumption lies behind this approach. Once men or institutions have been patched up, the problem will presumably vanish. According to the regnant ideas of progress and perfectability, this prevailing American view assumes that by conquering his environment, man will conquer himself. Ralph Barton Perry observed: "It would be American to improve and modernize Heaven rather than enjoy it for a static eternity." Whether by world government, world law, or a world religion, most moderns see man transfigured and the stubborn and imperfect human situation sent packing on its archaic way. Even early churchmen including those who are sometimes counted among the most austere and severe Calvinists of their day nonetheless faithfully mirror this typically American outlook. Thus Jonathan Edwards could say: "Providence intended America to be the renovator of the world."

A yet more recent religious departure from the Pauline view of man is found in the creed of the social gospel. The evangel of social action was in one sense a means of assuring that man would be unqualifiedly good through participation in the unremitting struggle for social justice and "the good." Yet those modernists who espoused the social gospel were saved from the worst illusions by their life in the real world. The defense of good required some of their goodness to rub off on the sources of social evil while the stubborn persistence of the Antichrist with whom they struggled kept alive a residual awareness of man's predicament.

It would be difficult to say the same for much postwar religious thinking. Positive thinking sees little need for man to transform himself. Rather he undertakes the transformation of others through suffering love and skilful use of divine forces that can be turned on and off through a controlling act of human will. Every man has at his beck and call spiritual forces that serve as a kind of divine messenger boy not alone for himself but for all those with whom he must come to terms, making selfish men generous, cruel men gentle, and ambitious men satisfied creatures. Every man can mobilize even on short notice spiritual energy to change men who obstruct the way to the good life. For this reason, the philosophy of the postwar religious revival has been called a spiritual version of the theory of progress. If the total culture is forever contriving ways to enable man to escape his struggle with himself, it is hardly surprising that religion too should create its own forms of escape.

Yet in the light of the harsh reality of history, it is clear that not one of these approaches, whether secular or religious, has prevented or forestalled a single great catastrophe of the age. For instance, none has prevented the rise of totalitarian democracy, the present cold war, or the continuing injustice in labor-management relations. Instead the various forms of anti-Pauline thought when their fruits become apparent lead to disillusionment, futility, and a sense of despair. By the test of experience, the wisdom of Paul's teachings are clear. One recalls Tennyson's familiar line: "Knowledge comes but wisdom lingers." The second limitation the Christian faces of sacrificing religion's central truths to powerful secular and supposedly religious currents of thought can be overcome only by recovering those truths. Burckhardt's reminder that the destruction of the good often lies within us is more pertinent as a referent than the call to do battle against this or that evil outside us which may in the end be imaginary or real. The Christian does face an unending struggle against nature and the world and he must move bravely to meet this challenge. Yet no less the struggle is always fundamentally one against his own baser nature, and this is the struggle present-day thought would have man forget or waft away through special pleading in the courts of heaven.

There is a final limitation—that of relating Christian standards for human conduct to the ambiguous associations of states. There are grounds for arguing that Christian standards have little if anything to do with the course states can pursue. Christianity calls for turning the other cheek. Was this a feasible rule to follow in relations with Hitler's Germany? The Gospel invites men to recompense evil with good. Are the lines of policy for a blockaded Berlin really suggested by this rule? Running through the New Testament is the doctrine of non-violence and the renunciation of force. Is this a valid guide in responding to the pressures from several hundred Russian divisions? Secretary of State Stimson in the early days of the postwar period announced a humane and morally appealing standard for dealing with the Russians when he observed that the way to have a friend was to be one. Has this proved to be an effective and realizable approach in the cold war? Since most honest observers of the international scene would in all candor answer these questions in negative terms, most Christian experts in international relations tend to reserve for religion a very modest place in guiding the conduct of states.

The conclusion, therefore, gains widespread acceptance as America's responsibilities have multiplied and the number of hard choices multiply, that at least in direct and explicit terms, Christian principles provide few rules or guides to action for foreign relations. Christian theologians like Reinhold Niebuhr and Christian laymen like George F. Kennan point out that attempts to apply such principles may even complicate the search for peace and security. Not the least of the problems stems from the intransigeance of Christian spokesmen when it comes to negotiating in areas of "principle." The ancient saying that men can compromise on interest but on principles never is a case at point. If foreign relations are viewed unqualifiedly as relations where right and wrong prevail and more especially when the right in every dispute is hedged about with divinity, tensions tend to become more extreme and less susceptible of accommodation.

Events leading up to the American Civil War are an example of the deterioration which sets in when each side views its case as a modern expression of the struggle for righteousness in which the prophets and apostles were engaged. When North and South saw the issue over slavery in scriptural terms, when they found the defense of their interests in holy writ, the democratic process of compromise and adjustment could no longer be made to work. For if men or nations view their cause as the full embodiment of right and virtue, there can be no concessions or adaptation to the other's cause or purpose. Hence the importing of religious precepts into the political arena may be more mischievous than constructive. This has led men whose personal lives were saintly to throw in doubt the place of religion when they turned to analyze international relationships.

If we turn from the Christian perspective for a moment to consider another limitation expressed in secular terms, the problem is much the same. Consider, for example, the relations of this country with non-democratic states. Every American President since George Washington has proclaimed the Republic's devotion to democracy here and abroad. One of our greatest Presidents, Woodrow Wilson, led the country in a holy crusade "to make the world safe for democracy." The Eisenhower Administration in 1952 rededicated itself to the liberation of subject peoples in eastern Europe from tyranny and oppression. By April 29, 1958, however, Vice-President Nixon, having been asked why the United States supported dictatorships in Latin America observed: "If we openly discriminate between one government and another in Latin America, what would we be charged with? We would be charged with interfering in the internal affairs of other countries and with trying to impose our system of government on them." Democracy is the practical moral choice of the American people after examining alternative forms of government. Clearly this is true for Mr. Nixon no less than

President Eisenhower or his forerunners. In practice, however, the application of a moral principle like support of democracy confronts serious obstacles the moment it finds its place alongside other principles like respect for the inviolable rights of a sovereign state.

Moral and religious perspectives applied to the behavior of states involve them in not one but two perplexing problems. The twin dilemma illustrated by the references to the American Civil War and our relations with Latin American dictatorships may be summarized as follows:

First, policies cloaked in religious and moral terms tend to become frozen, intractable, and absolute. Since a nation's or political party's policies must be interrelated and adjusted to another's, an absolute policy that is avowedly and self-consciously righteous and virtuous is less susceptible of change, compromise, and adaptation; since righteous men do not compromise virtue, two groups in conflict with each other cannot trim their claims in the interests of reducing the conflict. They can only hold their ground, defend what is right, and if necessary give of their blood and treasure in defense of principle. To recite this is of course not to say that for some international relationships the lines are not so clear that nations ought not to defend their rights precisely in these terms. I mean to imply only that policies and interests which are always justified and defended in Christian terms tend to increase world tensions and lead finally to a fatal conflict. Few wars that might have been prevented have been free of this tendency of states to see themselves in all they do as defenders of some "holy grail."

Second, the other form of the dilemma involved in the application of absolute principles has another cause. Policies of states entail not the application of a single principle but the balancing of several principles. A state may espouse the principle of collective security while at the same time being guided by the pursuit of peaceful settlement of disputes. Its goal may be the support of democracy around the world but it may also stand for recognition of the sovereign rights of other states to conduct their affairs and choose their form of government within their own borders. The balancing of these principles calls then for a kind of honest brokerage of principles. Prudence—not the principles themselves—must guide the balancing of these claims. The statesmen must turn then to an operating principle outside the contending moral principles. This is the art of politics and statecraft which while not denying the validity of moral principles must somehow bring about their reconciliation and accommodation. Because this is the context of international relationships, there is need for something more than the identification of what is the true and the good. If we explore the history of the relations of states, the great historic leaders and statesmen have been men who excelled in practical wisdom and prudence, which is to say, excelled in balancing moral principles. In considering the place of the Christian perspective in relations among states, this factor can never be overlooked.

3. Relevant Norms for the Cold War

What conclusions ought we to draw from the dilemmas and limitations of the Christian perspective in international relations? Is an awareness of these complexities and ambiguities grounds for rejecting the Christian message? Must cynicism and amorality be our response as we observe the gap between the purity of the religious story and the harsh truths of the world scene? Or are there areas in which the religious perspective retains its meaning and relevance? What can we say about the reconciliation of the "absolutely good" and "the immediately practical"? What, in short, does the Christian perspective have to say to the world of *Realpolitik?*

I believe there are at least five broad areas of relevance in

which ethical standards play a part which student or statesman, Christian or non-Christian can be asked to recognize.
First, I find a practical and valid role for Christian principles
in prompting states and peoples to recognize the qualities
all men share by virtue of being sons of God. All men possess
a common humanity the uniqueness of which resides in their
reflecting an image that is beyond man and history. In our
day there are signs throughout the world of a growing respect for human dignity even when partly abridged. Thus
in the year 1959, who would not rather be healthy than sick,
fed than hungry, housed than destitute or, capable of giving
their children a fair chance in life? One may say that these
are material needs and claims, yet their recognition bespeaks
a quickening of the human spirit everywhere. Obviously
vast differences persist in both desire and ability to reach
these goals but the almost universal search for a better life
tells us something about all mankind. Moreover, Christians
especially, who too easily become national Christians, do
well to recall the many lands that contribute to human
welfare. During World War II, Raymond Fosdick, then
President of the Rockefeller Foundation, wrote these un-
forgettable words:

An American soldier wounded on the battlefield in the Far
East owes his life to the Japanese scientist, Kitasato, who isolated
the bacillus of tetanus. A Russian saved by a blood transfusion
is indebted to Landsteiner, an Austrian. A German soldier is
shielded from typhoid fever with the help of a Russian, Metchni-
koff. A Dutch marine in the East Indies is protected from malaria
because of the experiments of an Italian, Grassi; while a British
aviator in North Africa escapes death from surgical infection because a Frenchman, Pasteur, and a German, Koch, elaborated a
new technique.
In peace as in war we are all of us the beneficiaries of contributions to knowledge made by every nation in the world. Our
children are guarded from diphtheria by what a Japanese and a
German did; they are protected from smallpox by an English-
man's work; they are saved from rabies because of a Frenchman;

they are cured of pellagra through the researches of an American. From birth to death they are surrounded by an invisible host— the spirits of men who never thought in terms of flags or boundary lines and who never served a lesser loyalty than the welfare of mankind.[39]

The horizons of our world view might be broader and our Christian insights deeper if we took this object lesson to heart.

Secondly, the church which teaches patience in all things should make it its business to inculcate this attitude toward world affairs. Someone has said that foreign affairs is singularly like a woman's work—it never ends. With the allure of novel institutions and procedures, the Christian like all Americans is all too ready to assume his problems can be resolved once and for all. However the United Nations buildings, multilingual translation systems, and instantaneous communications around the globe have not prevented one challenge or conflict from following close upon another. For example, a well-deserved and dearly won homeland for suffering and persecuted Jews has led to new and more fateful tensions in the Middle East; similarly, independence for the newer nations is only the beginning and not the end of their trials and tribulations. Walt Whitman wrote: "It is provided in the very essence of things that from any fruition of success, no matter what, shall come forth something to make a greater struggle necessary." Most of life is lived not on the mountain peaks of decisive triumphs but on plateaus of successive crises. Further, Christians particularly have occasion to remember that peace and prosperity in an "America sailing on a summer sea" never provide the acid test of character. Rather, true moral and spiritual resources are put to the test when loved ones depart, when peoples of nations teeter on the abyss of disaster, or when decisions have to be made on

[39] "The President's Review," *Annual Report of the Rockefeller Foundation for 1941*, p. 9.

which there is no present consensus nor any future certainty. In times like these strong persons or great leaders do not seek a convenient hiding place. A truly "positive faith" is not one which utters pleasurable platitudes in good times and holds its voice in bad times. Mankind will suffer all things provided there is someone who helps him chart his course through the storm and guides him with steady courage to a better day.

Third, American Protestants, particularly in a day when denominational strength is the primary goal, run the risk of sanctifying both the strengths and weaknesses of the national character. America's industry and trade, its cities and highways, its schools and welfare programs, attest to the vitality of the American creed of "growth and progress." Yet the United States, thrust suddenly onto the throne of world leadership, is both fortified and beset by its reforming zeal. Developments in other less favored countries yield slowly and often imperceptibly to our prompting and aid. Governments and societies in other lands are like plants; we are not their maker. Like a gardener we can patiently nurture them, tend and improve the soil, and pray for the grace of kindlier elements. But bursts of good intentions that light up the sky with impassioned exhortations to others to be as we are must remain as futile as the cries of the millennialists calling to God from the mountain top to come down and claim his own. Christians today must continually combat the temptation to believe that both God and men can be beguiled. A faith that rests on God's alacrity as a kind of personal messenger boy continually "on call" is as empty as a foreign policy that judges our friends by their dispatch in imitating American institutions. The world needs partners far more than patrons. It requires leaders who will search unremittingly for the concurrence of their own interests and the general welfare, and who are willing to accept the limits of their own cause in the quest for a higher one. Not selflessness, about which we prate so easily, but a richer selfhood should be the goal in which others are respected for their limits as well as their powers.

Fourthly, the Christian legacy has a special lesson for Americans living abroad. The American goal overseas is essentially one of translating the best in the missionary enterprise into secular terms. Foreign policy requirements set the magnitudes and locus of our aid; here the harsh imperatives of national interest must prevail. American resources are of course not unlimited. Their allocation is based on considerations of strategy and the potential economic and political development of those we aid. Once the choice has been made, however, the human side of technical assistance comes into play. Our human relations abroad are open to the "gentle civilizers" of mankind: religion, ethics, and the liberal values the West cherishes.

Christians who seek for an international equivalent of the clear moral issues that guide discriminations in the race question may, in at least one respect, find it in foreign aid. Man-to-man relations in the newer nations provide a severe test for the relevance of faith. When you are the grand benefactor and your friend is an humble supplicant the temptation to be less than Christian tests a living ethic to its roots. A good parent who sacrifices long and nobly for the welfare of his children runs a not inconsiderable risk of becoming obsessed with his own goodness and embittered when others are not persuaded. This is an almost daily problem in the underdeveloped areas for those who come bearing gifts and a new way of life.

Americans err if they view relations with newer nations primarily through the prism of frustrations, bewilderment, and failures in coming to terms with an alien culture. Religion, confronted with these difficulties, must have something to say about the incentives that cause men to leave safe havens for larger sacrifices, the moral resources that make them persist, and the wellspring that keeps compassion alive even in the face of ingratitude and evil. Living in alien cultures with peoples who are not American calls for patience and moral courage, compassion and understanding, steadfastness of purpose and unflinching resolve. Surely these are "Christian virtues" and an appropriate realm for the expression of the Christian perspective.

Finally, Christians should never forget—or let others forget—that we all live under God. He has judged us before we judged others. If the world sensed we believed as fervently that we too stood in judgment as we seem to believe in our own unquestioned righteousness, then perhaps the cry of hypocrisy, self-righteousness, and cant often directed against us might be moderated if not stilled. But even were those critics of America to persist, we ourselves might go forward with quiet assurance into the future. And if catastrophe were to befall, our moral resources for a time of troubles would be far greater than they are today.

Chapter Four

EPILOGUE: MORALISTS AND THE
INTERNATIONAL PROBLEM

I suspect that one reason for the present plight of political ethics in international relations is the relative impoverishment of contemporary thinking about the problem. I say this with no intention of belittling the spate of significant writing that crowds the reader's desk on a wide range of significant issues. The pages of the present abound in rich insights from serious philosophers, pundits, and former diplomats who advance understanding in ways too obvious for elaboration. However, those who are familiar with the overall contributions of most of this group need no reminder that their additions to knowledge are incidental to more general concerns and preoccupations. Mr. Kennan is primarily a diplomat and historian and Mr. Churchill primarily a statesman. Few of our contemporaries are basically political philosophers grappling with international morality in the sense that Aristotle, Plato, or Augustine were systematic writers on the ethics of the polity or the state. Instead the international polity has been the object of description, institutional analysis, and legal writing; reform movements have centered around the interests inherent in such approaches. The sword of Damocles suspended above most observers is the demand that they solve problems and do it promptly. There are students of ideologies, treaties, and emergent forms of international government; but who has written about "virtue" in international life? Who is the Socrates of international relations theory, and if we cannot find him is this accidental or a result of the harsh realities of world politics? Is it the nature of the international environment that inhibits a relevant "international moralizing" or is it the shortage of front-rank minds absorbed with the troublesome and baffling problems constantly arising in the world arena?

My thesis, which others can examine more fully and profoundly, is that both the nature of the international relations problem and the preoccupations of modern observers must be held accountable. Hans J. Morgenthau's *Dilemmas of Politics* illustrates the second aspect of this question. It reveals Professor Morgenthau as perhaps the greatest of our contemporary international theorists standing on the threshold of timeless political theory. It makes explicit the philosophy of a truly great mind—a philosophy which in earlier works has sometimes been largely implicit. It suggests to the present writer—and apparently to most reviewers—that with this study we are in the presence of a thinker whose philosophical equipment and political insights even now give evidence of placing him among those who belong to the ages. Yet Professor Morgenthau would be the first to offer two qualifications. First, the political theory of Hans J. Morgenthau is in process of unfolding. Unless I misread the aim and purpose of his intellectual journey, his final and most decisive treatise in political theory remains before him. Second, Professor Morgenthau has not said all he has to say about the relationship of religion, moral principles, and higher law to international politics. I believe this to be true because all the internal evidence points in this direction. If one reads and reflects, for example, on Professor Morgenthau's introduction to Ernest Lefever's challenging *Ethics and Foreign Policy,* one finds pointers and indeed a conceptual scheme that destroys—if this were necessary—the popular illusion that Morgenthau is solely a "power theorist."

Nevertheless, Morgenthau's "political theology" is in one sense at least unfinished business foreshadowed in *Scientific Man vs. Power Politics,* elaborated in *Dilemmas of Politics,* but not yet spelled out and given content in a form comparable to the writings of Augustine or Burke. And if this is true of the greatest of our contemporary writers on world politics, how much more is it true of lesser figures who at best must be considered political observers.

Beyond this, however, I believe the central problem is less the insufficiency of modern writings than it is the nature of the political and moral problem in international relations. The analysis of the "good life" in an integrated society founded on shared moral values is, comparatively speaking, a far simpler task than its discovery among autonomous moral communities. I can describe justice and righteousness within Britain or the United States. Constitutions, judicial opinions and legislation will guide me; the common good is roughly and approximately apparent. No such guides are at hand in the international order. The claims of this British leader or that American statesman to speak for the world evoke suspicion, hostility, and antagonism from those who see what is good for the world through their own national spectacles. One set of national purposes may at various points correspond to the general welfare but at countless other points diverge. This is the reason why sovereign groups find another's national moralizing so distasteful and pretentious. It is also the reason an extraordinarily able diplomatic tactician, John Foster Dulles, was not fully appreciated abroad until his final illness.

The one institution most capable of speaking for the world is the United Nations. It was founded on principles that inhere in the American constitution: social and political equality, a commitment to harmonize conflicting interests without warfare, concern for the welfare of all mankind, and devotion to the improvement of conditions capable of leading to conflict. The type of world to which the United Nations is dedicated is the kind of world in which American values might have a reasonable chance of surviving. Yet these objectives are basically the "symbolic" United Nations. This largest of all international organizations has demonstrated an ability to move toward fulfilling its goals through its actions in Korea, through the United Nations Emergency Force in the Middle East, and its social and economic endeavors around the globe. At the same time its modest successes or failures in Hungary, Kashmir, the Special United Nations Fund, and South West Africa remind us of its limitations and the fact that the symbolic United Nations is more a dream than a reality.

For the Secretary-General Dag Hammarskjold and the more realistic United Nations observers, the living United Nations is a cluster of procedures and an institutional framework for world diplomacy. There are those, including members of the Secretariat, who would have the Secretary-General signalize each achievement as a dramatic enactment of international values. They would have him state the permanent validity, say, of an international police force or of teams of United Nations Peace Observers. He by contrast has seen the need for a police force for the Gaza Strip while opposing one for Jordan or Berlin. Within the nation-state, institutional development often follows a straight line; the common law broadens out from precedent to precedent. Nothing of the sort characterizes the international order. Configurations of power and interest, time and place set limits to international action. If the United Nations were a genuine government advancing from strength to strength, the first worldwide experiment in collective security carried on in Korea would have laid the foundations for a response to the next challenge. In fact, the crisis in Indochina following close on Korea offers the classic answer to this fervent but wrongly held view. In Indochina as in Korea, the threat was the expansion of Communism across existing boundaries. But here as so often with international problems the parallel ceases. The Western allies whose unity at the center had made UN action possible in Korea were divided. The threat was more ambiguous, the virtue of the defenders of the status quo more beclouded, and their military capacity more in doubt. Support in the United Nations for a status quo that depended on the preservation of colonialism was out of the question from the beginning. Similarly with other crises, the challenge and the means of responding differ enough to restrict any automatic application of earlier UN techniques.

In the face of successive international crises each one in some way unique, the present Secretary-General has preferred to deal with problems on their merits. He has been the pragmatist par excellence not from design but because situations warranted it. His first objective has been to preserve the peace, and for this techniques and approaches have been the means to an end. The triumphs of Mr. Hammarskjold's period as Secretary-General have come less from the affirmation of broad international principles than from compromise and adjustment through quiet diplomacy. The United Nations is scarcely a means of eliminating the dilemmas of which I have spoken, even though in the hands of a deft and sensitive negotiator like Mr. Hammarskjold, it can be a means of living with such problems, blunting their sharpest edges and mitigating the tensions that might otherwise carry men over the brink of war.

Popular reformers and moralists sometimes argue that views on the nature of the international society such as I have been expounding are defeatist in character. They describe this approach as confused and offer easier and less painful resolutions of the problem. Thus the brilliant and scholarly Catholic theologian, Father John Courtney Murray, S.J., writes of the "disastrous tenet, that between morality and power a great gulf is fixed." [1] The issue between realists and idealists is an unreal issue which reason and logic can resolve if given half a chance. All the theorist need do is look for a middle ground between realism and idealism, between pacifism and bellicism. The problem, however, remains of finding the benign and salubrious middle ground in forms that go beyond its pious and abstract affirmation. The reader of Father Murray's tract will find little guidance in the realm of policy on problems like colonialism or diplomacy. One has the impression as with other distinguished Catholic writers that for him these issues evoke little concern. It is war in the form of military or ideological conflict that absorbs and inspires his attention. And here a cloak of rationalism enshrouds the analysis. As one of Father Murray's most perceptive critics has noted, he "is wholly right in warning us that conscience is not properly instructed by fear and anxiety. Fear and anxiety are very potent forces, and they vehemently assail the contemporary mind when it is engaged with the harrowing problems of war and survival. They must therefore be rigorously disciplined so that the mind can be adequately empowered and directed by the apprehension of the real good. True. But the truth tempts us to sell short a fact or two, such as the very deep fear that the family of nations is a wolf pack rather than a human community. . . ." [2] Put another way, the international society is made up of human communities each assuming a monopoly of political and moral virtue.

It is not by accident, I believe, that Father Murray and his friends are intrigued by the thesis argued so forcefully by Henry A. Kissinger in *Nuclear Weapons and Foreign*

---

[1] John Courtney Murray, S.J., *Morality and Modern War* (New York: The Church Peace Union, 1959), p. 21.

[2] Julian N. Hartt, "Religion and the Bomb," *Worldview*, II, No. 4 (April 1959), 7. Successive issues of this valuable little journal provide a continuing discussion of our subject.

Policy. The notion is appealing that nuclear warfare can be carried on with small thermonuclear weapons and military targets and zones clearly differentiated and observed. History offers some consolation to the followers of this viewpoint but it also provides damaging examples of states that refused to restrict their employment of ultimate weapons when the stakes were sufficiently high. Professor Hartt points out: "Father Murray has not . . . clearly enough come to terms with the question behind every serious consideration of limited war as a moral option, i.e., where are the ethical principles to fix the appropriate limits? *Where,* not *what:* can we make out the lineaments of the community which is the living repository (as it were) of the ethical principles relevant and efficacious to the moral determination of the limits of warfare." [3] He concludes that such a community is lacking.

It is fair to ask whether any limited-war doctrine does justice to the depth of the moral problem in ignoring the essential character of the present-day international environment. If state behavior were as rational and moral as Father Murray assumes it must be to prevent mutual annihilation once conflict breaks out, the ambiguities of international politics in areas short of war would be less persistent and intractable than they are. He recognizes this in his anxious concluding phrase: "moral principles cannot impart [a] sense of direction to power until they have first . . . passed through the order of politics. . . ." [4] Yet the order of international politics antecedent to war which preoccupies the bulk of the writers we have called into play concerns Father Murray hardly at all in his zeal to moralize military doctrine.

An opposite approach that has wide support among Protestant believers is that of the saintly theologian and missionary, Albert Schweitzer. He maintains that "in a very general sense, ethics is the name we give to our concern for

[3] *Ibid.*
[4] Murray, *op. cit.,* p. 20.

good behavior. We feel an obligation to consider not only our own personal well-being but also that of others and of human society as a whole." [5] The beginnings of ethics can be found in the birth of a sense of solidarity with others. Primitive man is restricted to tribal and blood loyalties; civilization gradually widens the circle to encompass the world. "As man starts reflecting upon himself and his behavior toward others, he gradually realizes that all men are his brothers and neighbors." [6] The great religions and philosophies have prompted this awareness. Sometimes they are frustrated in their quest for universal brotherhood by the impediments of stubborn notions of class barriers (Brahmanism), holy wars against infidels (Zarathustra), freemen and slaves (early Greek philosophy), detachment from the problems of the world (early Christianity), or non violence leading to abstention from evil rather than affirmation of the good (Buddhism). Christianity initially exhorted men to seek the perfection required for participation in the kingdom of God. They awaited and expected the transformation of the world. "When Christianity became more familiar with the enthusiastic affirmation of the world, which the Renaissance had bequeathed to European thought, it at the same time became reacquainted with ethical Stoicism and noted with surprise that Jesus' principle of Love had also been stated as a rational truth." [7] Erasmus and Grotius are thinkers who were loyal both to Christianity and Stoicism. The blending of Christianity and philosophy led to an era of practical morality. The ethics of Love could no longer rest easy with injustice, cruelty, and superstition. Altruism was rationalized and for eighteenth-century philosophers like Holbach and Bentham was grounded in the principle of utility. Kant and Hume refuted the utilitarian doctrine by substituting re-

[5] Albert Schweitzer, "The Evolution of Ethics," *The Atlantic Monthly*, CCII, No. 5 (Nov. 1958), 69.
[6] *Ibid.*
[7] *Ibid.*, p. 71.

spectively the categorical imperative and the concept of sympathy and compassion. For Kant: "We have to obey the moral law that we carry within ourselves to gain the certitude that we not only belong to the world as it appears to us in time and space, but that we are at the same time citizens of the spiritual world." [8] For Hume, nature has "endowed us with the faculty of sympathy, which obliges us to feel the joy, apprehensions, and sufferings of others as if they were our own." [9] After Hume, few philosophies dare assume that ethics is not primarily a matter of compassion.

How does one give content to the ethics of compassion? For Schweitzer by a "reverence for life." The fundamental idea of the conscience is: "I am life wanting to live, surrounded by life wanting to live. Meditating upon life, I feel the obligation to respect any will-to-live around me as equal to mine and as having a mysterious value." [10] Schweitzer recognizes the numerous disturbing conflicts society faces in applying his creed. "We are constantly in situations which compel us to harm other creatures or affect their lives. The farmer cannot let all his animals survive. He can keep only those he can feed and the breeding of which assures him necessary income. In many instances, there is the obligation of sacrificing some lives to save others. Whoever shelters a crippled bird finds it necessary to kill insects to feed him." [11] Nevertheless, it is "incumbent upon each of us to judge whether we must harm or kill, and thus become, by necessity, guilty." [12]

Schweitzer's matchless contribution both in his life and his words is to heighten and intensify ethical sensitivity. When he implies, however, that men can and must exemplify these precepts as part of an evolving ethics, he offers a

[8] *Ibid.*, p. 72.
[9] *Ibid.*
[10] *Ibid.*, p. 73.
[11] *Ibid.*, p. 72.
[12] *Ibid.*

towering moral standard that all must respect but few can attain. The conflicts he describes but then sets aside with exhortations that a civilized world must perish unless they are fulfilled are even more intense and far-reaching than he recognizes. What are we to say of military preparation on which national security rests? Are the moral perils and the casualties of human life which attend every military training program to be condemned outright? Or is the sacrifice of life and sacred treasure to assure that the values he cherishes will live as morally inferior as his trend of thought would indicate? Are the Schweitzers of each age enabled to teach and minister because the threat of barbarism and tyranny has been arrested by those who took human life before finally yielding up their own in the cause of civilization and decency? Is not the pathos of international life far deeper than the realm of animal and insect life, given the call for courage which, no less than compassion, is essential to civilization's survival? Are the hard choices more ineradicable than Schweitzer's discussion of the evolution of ethics implies, especially if we picture the line of ascent as moving ever upward from narrow tribal loyalties in primitive life to the whole of mankind in the modern world?

I should not wish to disparage the moral grandeur of Schweitzer's religious philosophy. I would only suggest that his philosophy has greater immediate relevance for interpersonal ethics than for the half-jungle world of international relations. When he traces history's purifying effect on the evolution of ethics, he speaks more convincingly to the problem of man's relation to man than to the "law" of relations among states. In fact, there have been periods in history where universalism was more pervasive than our own. Today values and devotion are locked up far more than some might wish in sovereign nation states, each essentially a law unto itself.

The trouble with Father Murray and Mr. Schweitzer is

that they represent for international relations opposite extremes on a spectrum. Father Murray's is essentially a hard moralism while Mr. Schweitzer represents, for the international realm at least, a soft moralism. Their views are immensely instructive and important in the limited but important areas for which they have relevance. Father Murray's "intermediate" doctrine of war reminds us that in public policy this country has increasingly prepared solely for a type of absolute warfare that is neither moral nor rational. As a nation, we are geared to fight only the kind of battles that present no true moral option. But a moral doctrine that has relevance only to warfare is at best an incomplete moral approach. Father Murray has taken war as the extreme case and is therefore both oblivious and a little contemptuous of moral approaches short of that. At the opposite pole Mr. Schweitzer holds up a warning sign to a civilization that runs the risk of being terrifyingly casual about the mystery and preciousness of human life. All of us as individuals would do well to ponder our own attitude and reverence toward life. While I doubt that for most men engaged, for example, in eradicating insects that wreak havoc on other forms of life, a sense of guilt must accompany their acts, I would agree that wanton destruction of life to no constructive purpose was unquestionably evil. However, man's calculated decision to take life that others may live, as in scientific laboratories, is a relatively simple example of the paradoxes that arise. Is the sacrifice of animal life to bring about new ways of preserving human life too great a price to pay? How does one apply Schweitzer's concept here? The world of Albert Schweitzer's African mission is relatively simple and uncomplicated compared to the world of states, each contending for security, influence, and prestige. For international affairs, in the same way that love cannot always be translated directly into guides for action, reverence for life raises many problems with which the sensitive conscience must grapple.

Both Father Murray and Albert Schweitzer have stated principles that are worthy of the most serious and prayerful reflection. Neither has seen fit in any comprehensive way to apply their principles to the vast realm of world affairs. If they had, I could imagine both grappling with the "hard cases" in much the way Judge de Visscher, Geoffrey Barraclough, or Chester I. Barnard struggle to come to terms with reality. Since neither moralist has taken this tack, their importance for international relations must in the large appear minimal to those who search for truth.

I have dwelt on the problem of hard and soft moralism and certain representative approaches because many see in them the solution to some of the moral riddles with which this volume is concerned. If the international problem were less intractable, these writings would probably suffice. When the scholar looks more closely at their contribution, however, he turns sadly but of necessity again to philosophers like Niebuhr and Butterfield. Nonetheless the illusion is widespread that men like Schweitzer offer answers that would enable us to transcend the dilemmas of foreign policy. I find little in the text of their writings to substantiate this, however much one may draw of inspiration and guidance in forming one's personal ethic.

Therefore, the realistic moralist must return to the problems with which we began—problems of power, of the gulf between individual and collective morality, and of the relation of national interest to higher aims and purposes. In our lifetime these issues will undoubtedly persist; they form the context in and for which relevant standards must be derived. Unhappily progress and the evolution of ethics have left wide reaches of international behavior relatively untouched. The Christian ethicist would have reason to assume this was true and in the end he may therefore be better equipped to deal with reality. He must never use this fact to excuse indifference or acceptance of things as they are. Historically, he has always found himself in tension with society; standards of love, justice, and forgiveness place him forever at odds with cruelty, injustice, and a politics of revenge. Yet he has never been completely free to practice the law of love or the doctrine of reverence for life. These pure truths must pass through the filter of circumstances which he can work to improve but can never perfect.

Knowing this, those of us who stand on the sidelines in the unending drama of world politics may perhaps achieve a greater measure of compassion and understanding. We may be more tolerant of those who must act and not merely philosophize. In this way, we the people may perhaps be purged of some of the self-righteousness and superiority that alienates policy-makers and the public and sets man against man in debates on what is true and just. We might all in the end be more moral if a sense of cosmic humility rather than self-conscious righteousness informed what we said and did. This is my chief excuse for discussing at such length and with the aid of so many earnest and sincere thinkers Christian Ethics and the Dilemmas of Foreign Policy.

Index

146 INDEX

necke on, 45-46, 47, 49-50; moralism, compared with, 4, 26-27, 42-43, 58-59, 99, 100-102, 137-144; and political realism, 37-38; and politics, 12, 50, 98-99; private and public, 48-49, 98-99; proximate standards of, 27-28; reformism and, 47-49; science, compared with, 11, 43; self-righteousness in, 57

Morgenthau, Hans J., 133-134

Morison, Dr. Robert S., and views on social science, 6-7

Munro, Sir Leslie, 85

Murray, Father John Courtney, S.J., 137-138, 142, 143

National interest, 21, 22, 23, 35-36, 41-42, 44, 59; dimensions of, 41-42; limits of, 26, 40

Nation state: and moral impulses, 15; and nationalism, 13, 20-21; and national loyalties, 20-21; need for transformation of, 16; sources of unity within the, 14

Natural law: and consent, 11; and Grotius, 10 ff; in the Middle Ages, 9; and Nuremberg trials, 12; and positive law, 11; rejection by contemporary west, 15

Negotiations: and moral principles, 37-38; and the old diplomacy, 81-82

Nehru, Prime Minister Jawaharlal, 54, 86

Nicolson, Sir Harold, 89, 116

Niebuhr, Reinhold: before World War I, 17; on Christianity and democracy, 23; on idealism and realism, 3, 25-26; on individual and group egoism, 20-21; on international organization, 22; on man, 17, 18, 19; on the Marshall Plan, 21; on mass society, 20; on morality, proximate and ultimate, 27-28; on national interest, 21, 26, 27; on political theory, 17; on power, 19; on statesmanship, 21; on UNESCO, 22; on universal law, 26; writings of, 17

North Africa, and national universities, 14

North Atlantic Treaty Organization, 35

Nuremberg trials, 12

On Liberty, 4

Outlawry of war, 15

Pacifism, 27, 28, 38-40

Papacy: and international law, 8; and international state, 9; and moral dilemma, 10; and *plenitudo potestatis*, 9

Pearson, Lester B., 87

Perry, Ralph Barton, 121

Physical sciences, purpose in, 5

Plato, 8

Plenitudo potestatis, 9

Political theory: definitions of, 7; according to Reinhold Niebuhr, 17

Politics: Churchill on, 31-34; compromise in, 36; conflict in, 59-60; and force, 31-33; and group loyalties, 20; and human nature, 18; and international law, 13-15; and the law of love, 27-28; Thomas Molnar on, 51; and political judgment, 29; and prudence, 34-35; and security-power dilemma, 19-20, 59-60; tension with morality, 50

Positive law: in the Middle Ages, 10; in Pufendorf, 12; relation to natural law, 11

Power: Churchill on, 31-34; and force, 31-32; Niebuhr on, 18; and politics, 20; security-power dilemma, 19; and statesmanship, 22-23

Pufendorf, 8, 12

Religion: and economics, 94; and political loyalties, 20

Research, and theory, 5

Ricardo, 7

Roosevelt, Franklin Delano: on colonialism, 76; and personal diplomacy, 86

Rusk, Dean, 85-86

Russell, Lord Bertrand, 110, 115

Saint Paul, 117-118

Schweitzer, Albert, 138-143

Science: unity of, 5; Churchill on, 29-31; differences between social and physical, 5; and morality, 11, 43

Science, American, and Soviet threat, 14

Scientist, laboratory, and purpose, 6

Secularism: and Christianity, 23, 24; and democracy, 23, 24

Security: dilemma, 19; man's quest for, 19; primacy of, 22

Shotwell, James, 79-80